Amber delivers a proven pathway to guide our best and brightest educators towards their potential in the classroom and beyond. No longer will frustration, isolation, or burnout strip the educational field of top-notch teaching talent. Learning how to achieve a Burned-In perspective and lifestyle allows educators to positively impact students for generations to come. This is a must-read for every level of educator!

— GRETCHEN BRIDGERS, OWNER AT ALWAYS A LESSON; TEACHER, TRAINER, AND COACH; AUTHOR OF *ELEMENTARY EDUC 101: WHAT THEY DIDN'T TEACH YOU IN COLLEGE*

Hacking Teacher Burnout utilizes the power of personal narrative to shed light on the incredible social-emotional capacities demanded of educators in the classroom today. In essence, *Hacking Teacher Burnout* humanizes a profession that has become so dehumanized by things like standardized testing and developmentally inappropriate state standards and shows us that in order to nurture and support our students as human beings, we must nurture and support ourselves. Compassion isn't a pie with limited slices to dole out. Rather, when we show compassion towards ourselves, we find that there's even more compassion to offer towards our students and each other. The courage and vulnerability of Amber Harper and her eight powerful "life hacks" in this revolutionary text add an unprecedented level of clarity to understanding the issue of teacher resilience and self-care.

— DANNA THOMAS, HAPPY TEACHER REVOLUTION

After eighteen years in education, I've had my shares of ups and downs, and yes, even burnout. *Hacking Teacher Burnout* is relevant, timely, and beneficial for educators at any stage. As I read through *Hacking Teacher Burnout* from the perspective of an instructional coach and now a principal, the strategies and tips were so impactful that I started taking notes and wishing the book was included in university courses for teachers. As Amber explains, overcoming burnout isn't just about getting your heart back in the game; it's about cultivating the best you. If you decide that teaching is where you're meant to be and you implement the action steps outlined in the book, you will wake up with a purpose, have an upgraded zest for teaching, improve your relationships, and your soul will smile as you show up ready to share your strengths with the world. Burnout doesn't have to define you, keep you stuck, or leave you feeling hopeless. That life you've been wanting—it does exist, and it is within reach. Read on, and we'll be on the lookout for your sparkle.

— JEN MOLITOR, INSTRUCTIONAL COACH, AUTHOR OF *THE HAPPY TEACHER'S HANDBOOK: FROM OVERWHELMED TO INSPIRED—HELPING TEACHERS EMBRACE RESILIENCY*

HACKING
TEACHER BURNOUT

8 STEPS TO GO FROM ISOLATED TO EMPOWERED SO YOU CAN OVERCOME ANY CHALLENGE

 HACK™
Learning
SERIES

AMBER HARPER

Hacking Teacher Burnout
© 2020 by Times 10 Publications

These books are available at special discounts when purchased in quantity for premiums, promotions, fundraising, and educational use. For inquiries and details, contact us at 10Publications.com.

Published by Times 10
Highland Heights, OH
10Publications.com

Cover and Interior Design by Steven Plummer
Editing by Carrie White-Parrish
Copyediting by Jennifer Jas

Library of Congress Cataloging-in-Publication Data is available.
ISBN (paperback): 978-1-948212-22-9
ISBN (eBook): 978-1-948212-58-8
First Printing: September, 2020

Dedicated to all teachers who have suffered through challenges alone.

TABLE OF CONTENTS

FOREWORD

ALWAYS KNEW I wanted to become a teacher. I dressed in my dad's oversized T-shirts and my mom's high heels and taught my stuffed animals in our formal living room. Every Christmas growing up, I was given items for my future classroom (books to read, cutesy office supplies, teacher swag, and more).

When I finally opened the door of my very first classroom, though, I never could have imagined what waited for me only a few years later. I was bright-eyed and full of creative ideas to bring my lessons to life for my students. I was not prepared for the three main hardships I would encounter: 1) teaching Title 1 students, 2) being in a school where more than 80 percent of the population qualified for free and reduced lunch, and 3) experiencing extremely limited parental involvement. My undergraduate program did not prepare me for these factors. So when I experienced them, my lifelong dreams of what teaching would be like slowly deflated and became instead teaching survival techniques paired with multiple grade levels of content to meet my students' needs.

I was burned-out before I even knew it.

I loved teaching. I loved my kids. I did *not* love the emotions and stress that came from either of those things. I was unprepared … and I was under-supported. I was a strong instructional leader in my classroom, but I was not well-versed in managing the emotions that began to stir within me.

I knew I had to do something, though, so I applied for a position at a neighborhood school during our transfer fair period. I felt overwhelmed with guilt for leaving the kids that needed me most. But if I did not take care of myself first, I'd never make the impact I needed and wanted to make in the educational field. At the time, I knew it all had to start with a change of scenery. So I moved to a suburban elementary school with high parental involvement.

After a period of culture shock and learning how to navigate new obstacles and opportunities, I was back in action.

I was a natural leader. I had a student teacher my third year into my career—a tad too early, in my opinion, but I rose to the challenge. Every year after that, I was given multiple opportunities to lead teachers, whether it was mentoring my peers, leading professional development sessions, or developing the new teacher support program schoolwide.

I had never felt more fulfilled. I realized that the one season of burnout I experienced—and the changes I made because of it—had completely changed the trajectory of my life. During that burnout phase, I could have hung up my teacher hat and changed careers. The emotional toll it took on my mind and body nearly stole my joy for what I always wanted to be when I grew up. If I'd quit, though, I would have missed out on the rewards that came after it. Thank goodness I prioritized my well-being so I could fall in love with teaching all over again. For the next few years, I led students and staff to new levels of achievement and proficiency. But another season of burnout was on its way.

I couldn't put my finger on the cause, but I recognized that burnout feeling immediately when it appeared. *Oh no. Not again!* I thought. I didn't want to leave my new school; I enjoyed the new environment and challenges.

Still, I couldn't lie to myself. I was thriving, but I was miserable.

How could those two things even coexist? I taught literacy to multiple classes every day. I led a large team of colleagues who were facing numerous personal obstacles and professional struggles. I provided professional development for my school and district.

And I was burnt out. All those spinning plates in the air were about to crash down if I didn't make a change. Rather, a choice.

An email arrived in my inbox, asking if I was interested in coaching new teachers in our district, grades K–12. I had thought that being a classroom teacher was what I had always wanted to be and do, but this new position taught me that teaching others was where my passion lived. Now it looked like I had the opportunity to teach teachers—something I had been doing for years. Even better, I wouldn't have to teach a class and complete all the other tasks of a classroom teacher while I did it.

I said yes … and I had the time of my life being an instructional coach for The New Teacher Project with TEACH Charlotte. I hadn't even known that role existed in education. I thought you were either a teacher or an administrator. But the hybrid role felt like home. I grew in leaps and bounds in my instructional knowledge and execution while building relationships with countless educators.

At that point, I had escaped burnout twice. Not because I was special, but because I made choices. Choices that helped me move forward and reset rather than getting stuck and quitting. And here's a secret: you can do the same thing, as many times as you need to.

When I had my own experiences, I didn't have the benefit of knowing Amber or her mission to support teachers facing their own versions of burnout. I met her when I transitioned my coaching practice from working for a company to working for myself.

That was when everything became clear regarding what happened to me and why.

Amber is knowledgeable and relatable and a rock-solid support system. We became instant friends as we swapped stories about our burnout and how we turned our passion projects for helping educators into full-time missions. We loved what we did and who we did it for. It was empowering, and we couldn't be happier that we stuck through our seasons of burnout so that we could experience the rewards on the other side.

The more we talked, the more I realized that burnout was a signal for change, not a death sentence.

A lot of healing can happen for you, too, if you take the time to follow Amber's guidelines. Her *Teacher Burnout* Hacks create an empowering roadmap to build momentum for where you want to go in your future as an educator. Had I had access to this resource when I was facing my seasons of burnout, I could have:

- Had a better understanding of what was happening and why

- Felt more confident about making a challenging choice that was aligned with what I needed and wanted

- Had a strong woman alongside me, cheering me on to continue chasing my dreams

- Shortened my season of burnout immensely, with Amber as my guide

I couldn't be happier for you to have Amber's support, as I know it could have been a game-changer for me. Now, when an educator I lead starts to show signs of burnout, I immediately point them toward Amber. I know how much her proven method can improve an educator's career and student achievement.

Please know one thing. Just because things are hard doesn't mean you can't face them. It means you are getting shined up to become a better, more polished version of yourself. It's a welcomed obstacle that can work for you if you let it.

Had I not felt burned-out at my first school, I would never have found my next school, which provided more learning opportunities for me to hone my craft. Had I not felt burned-out at my second school, I would never have blossomed into someone who now coaches new teachers up to teacher leaders. The only reason I have a varied classroom experience of grade level and student population is because of burnout. And the only reason I have varied leadership experience of teacher proficiency and titles is because of burnout. It forced me to do the work to change my situation and get into a better, more beneficial reality.

Burnout blessed me with a more fulfilling career than I ever dreamed about as I taught my stuffed animals while I wore my dad's oversized T-shirt and my mom's high heels.

Get honest with yourself. Take risks. Trust the process. And allow your potential to rise.

Hacking Teacher Burnout will save you once you hit burnout and also help prevent it from ever taking you out. The eight Hacks are practical tips that you can apply personally and professionally, as often as necessary, to get yourself back on track when you feel burnout looming.

You are never stuck in your situation unless you choose to stay in the mud and muck.

Read the book.

Do the work.

Interact in the community.

You can still achieve the dream you held for yourself when you started teaching that very first year, even with burnout as part of your story. It's a chapter in your book … but it's not the whole book.

The possibilities are endless, and the BURNED-IN version of you awaits.

Go be great!

— GRETCHEN BRIDGERS, OWNER OF ALWAYS A LESSON; TEACHER, TRAINER, AND COACH; AUTHOR OF *ELEMENTARY EDUC 101: WHAT THEY DIDN'T TEACH YOU IN COLLEGE*

PROLOGUE
HOW THIS BOOK RELATES TO THESE TIMES

*H*ACKING TEACHER BURNOUT *was in the works long before the Coronavirus pandemic and the necessary surfacing of the social justice movement. These times have made this book and this topic even more compelling and timely. The Prologue and Epilogue shine a light on the ongoing epidemic of teacher burnout in the context of current events.*

Val had been a teacher for fifteen years, and although she'd had her ups and downs (as everyone has in their career), nothing prepared her for the current crisis: teaching from home during the Coronavirus global pandemic.

She wasn't new to technology, and she previously used it with her fourth graders, but when their school was ordered to close for the remainder of the school year in March 2020, it forced her and her twenty-eight students to go virtual.

Plans seemed to change by the day, and at first, Val rolled with the punches, planning and replanning her strategy for satisfying her district's needs and her kids' needs. In the past, she'd had a pretty good relationship with her administrators, but their lack of planning and sticking with it started to create high stress in her daily life. With every email from her principal, she learned about a new change or a new expectation she had to meet.

Val was also a mom of three children: Thomas (fourteen years old), Kayla (eight years old), and Hadley (two years old), and although Thomas was pretty self-sufficient with his virtual learning, Kayla needed consistent help understanding her assignments. With Hadley not being able to go to daycare, she needed constant attention and was getting more and more stir-crazy as the days passed.

Jeff, Valerie's husband, was working from home as well, and his demanding daily schedule of Zoom meetings, paperwork, and deadlines kept him from being consistent with his help with the kids. Therefore, Val had to turn to Thomas to help with Kayla and Hadley. She experienced tremendous mom guilt about asking her oldest son to care for her younger children so she could answer emails, call parents, and do the daily and weekly lesson planning, preparing, and executing.

Val had already been struggling with feeling overwhelmed since Hadley was born, and she was struggling to balance all she had to do to be a good teacher to her growing number of students each year. Now this.

Although she put out lesson videos and assignments and felt like she was doing a decent job of getting a handle on this "virtual teaching" thing, only half of her twenty-eight students participated. She was worried about a couple of her students who needed a lot of support; they weren't involved in the virtual lessons. She was even more concerned when she couldn't get in touch with their families.

She answered emails, phone calls, and questions from parents on social media at all hours of the day and was now up to about eleven hours a day of work, sometimes answering emails in the middle of the night.

How was she supposed to be a good mom and teacher at the same time? How could she possibly reach all her students' needs when she hadn't seen or heard from some of them in weeks? How was she supposed to set up clear boundaries while teaching from home when she couldn't even establish them when she had been in the classroom?

Val had no idea how she could keep up this pace. She even considered quitting teaching; she wondered, even after this passed, what would be next.

Val, like many teachers, desperately needed to Hack Teacher Burnout.

INTRODUCTION
SET YOURSELF UP FOR SUCCESS, EVEN WHEN HARDSHIP IS GUARANTEED

THINK BACK TO when you first started teaching. Before you even stepped foot in your first classroom. You knew you wanted to make an impact. You knew you wanted to empower students with the gift of knowledge so they could achieve their goals in life.

But then something happened. *Many* things happened. Whether from paperwork, challenging students, or an even more challenging policy or leader, you began to burn out. You felt left behind, pushed too far—or worse, like you didn't matter at all. You began to feel disempowered, unworthy, and incapable of changing anything—because the very system you wanted to be a part of so badly had changed you, and not in a good way.

You don't need this book to know that teacher burnout is a

problem and that your desire for change and support is real. You're looking for real, strategic ways to change your current reality and, ultimately, change your life for the better.

You likely know that teacher job satisfaction has dropped fifteen points since 2009, from 59 percent of teachers claiming to be very satisfied in 2009 to 44 percent in 2020. Forty-four percent satisfaction is the lowest level in over twenty years. According to the U.S. Department of Education, the percentage of teachers who say they are very or fairly likely to leave the profession has increased by 12 points since 2009, from 17 percent to 29 percent.

When I created BURNED-IN Teacher in April of 2016, I did so because I wanted to offer action, inspiration, and support to teachers dealing with burnout and allow them a safe space for sharing their stories without being met with judgment or negativity.

I wanted to create a place where, whether the challenge or change was large or small, teachers could turn, trust, and relate to each other. A place that would help them thrive through the hardship. BURNED-IN then became the eight-step process and system it is today. One that gives teachers a place to turn when their reality seems dark and impossible. A place where they can find the tools they need to get themselves back on the right track.

As I've gone through burnout myself, studied it, and worked with teachers struggling through their seasons of burnout, I've learned that tackling it is not as simple as a standard one-size-fits-all solution. Too often, we try Band-Aids, but we are putting them on gaping wounds that require more than a bottle or three of wine to numb them. Teachers face all different types of burnout, and solutions can be as complex as the individuals seeking them.

Chances are, you've been through a challenge that rocked you. You've felt the effects of this occupational phenomenon called burnout. You have YouTubed, Googled, and read about the signs and symptoms and the call to put on your oxygen mask before helping others.

If you scroll through Twitter, Instagram, or Facebook, you will find comedic videos, images, gifs, and memes that glorify the struggle teachers go through every day. They're hilarious because they resonate with us, but the fact is, they point out an issue. Teaching is hard, and it gets more difficult each year. And though laughter is great medicine, it's also only good for the short term. After the smile fades and the laughter stops, you're still returning to business as usual. Stress. Exhaustion. Frustration. Burnout.

Sometimes, the shame that surrounds burnout also keeps us silent and isolated, and those roots can run deep, keeping us stuck— or telling us that the only way out is to quit. But that's not always the case.

Why are some teachers able to create a life they love while teaching, while others live day to day and just go through the motions, feeling like they're barely keeping their heads above water? Why do some teachers thrive while others feel like they're just surviving? And why are some educators able to keep teaching happily for the duration of their career, while others burn out after just a few years?

Hacking Teacher Burnout will help you find the line between feeling fulfilled and barely surviving, so you will be aware when you are getting close to the line and can take steps to stay on the fulfilled side. This book will help you navigate those challenges and crises and give you actionable steps to allow you to acknowledge, prepare for, and thrive through the hardships. I'll teach you to build a solid vision for your personal and professional life when things get hard.

As you make your way through the Hacks, know that the goal is to help you find fulfillment. If you're feeling ready to get out of education, read this book before you decide. I'm going to help you take specific action steps that are best for *you*, depending on your burnout type and your personal and professional goals.

If you're looking for a manual about becoming someone you're not, to please people you don't like, in a place you hate being, then this isn't the book for you. *Hacking Teacher Burnout* isn't about faking life as you smile through your misery. It's about perspective, mindset, vision, and small steps you can take daily to create a happier, more fulfilled life on your terms—no matter what the challenge or crisis. Everyone's steps are different sizes and go in different directions. This book will not dictate your steps, but it will guide them.

No matter where or what you teach, consider this your permission slip to be a happy, healthy, fulfilled human being.

Hacking Teacher Burnout is divided into eight steps or Hacks that spell the eight letters of BURNED-IN. Each Hack builds on the others, helping you to act on your burnout and reflect on what you're thinking and doing. I don't suggest putting this book on the shelf after you've read it once, either. Changing your habits takes time, practice, grace, and patience. Even after Hack 1, you may realize that the idea of *Hacking Teacher Burnout* sounds simple, yet it is far from easy. It requires soul-searching, self-awareness building, and action-taking. You will figure out why you're burned-out in the first place, what you truly want, and how you can get there.

The eight Hacks in the process will guide you as you take this journey. They are meant to go through again and again, any time you face a challenge in your career or life and need to center and empower yourself to focus and move forward. You will find ways to assess your specific burnout triggers, build your self-awareness, address your biggest challenges, seek and find the support you need to solve them, decide what you truly want from your career, and take daily action toward your goals.

Think of these Hacks as stepping stones or landmarks on your journey out of isolation and burnout and into becoming an empowered teacher.

As with the other books in the *Hack Learning Series*, each chapter presents easy-to-follow strategies under these section headings: The Problem, The Hack, What You Can Do Tomorrow, A Blueprint for Full Implementation, Overcoming Pushback, and The Hack in Action.

In this book, you'll learn how to go from a burned-out educator to a BURNED-IN human. But it starts with you knowing where you are in your burnout. Therefore, before Hack 1, you should know two things about yourself:

1. Your Teacher Burnout Type

2. Your Burnout Stage (how burned-out you are)

What Burnout Type Are You?

Burned and Over It? Burned and Unbalanced? Or Burned and Bored?

You Might Be a *Burned and Over It* Teacher If:

You've been battling burnout (whether you knew it or not) in isolation for too long. You're now so apathetic to your work that you don't see the point in being in your classroom every day. You lack connection to everyone around you.

You don't know why you're in education anymore and don't know what to do or where to start to fix the way you feel. You're not sure you even *want* to fix it if it means continuing in education.

You may find yourself saying things like, "No matter how hard I work, I'll be disappointed with the results." You used to love teaching, going to school, and interacting with students, their parents, your administrator, and staff. But now you couldn't care less about interaction and usually avoid it.

You Might Be a *Burned and Unbalanced* Teacher If:

You love teaching, just not all the extras you've committed to handling. Now you're at a crossroads: Either you keep trying to do all the things you've committed to doing and living up to the expectations you and your school have put on you, risking a nervous breakdown, or you make changes. But how? You may find yourself saying things like, "I used to love being so involved in leading clubs, teams, and other committees in my school, but I'm exhausted. I just want to do my job as a teacher and go home. I used to be okay with grading at night and on weekends, but it's gotten out of hand."

You feel that when you started teaching, you were happy to take on extra responsibilities, either because you had the spare time or because you were simply happy to do it. You didn't mind putting in the extra hours of planning, prepping, grading, and entering. But now, you're starting to see what you're missing out on because of all of your responsibilities.

You Might Be a *Burned and Bored* Teacher If:

You feel that you need a challenge in your professional life. Something new. Something that will push you to learn new things, meet new people, or go to new places. But you're consistently at odds with yourself. You feel that you should be happy with your situation, but you just aren't anymore. Where do you start, and how do you take back control while challenging yourself?

You may be thinking things like, "I still love education and teaching, but I'm bored with what I'm doing. My students deserve someone passionate about this grade and subject. I need to find something that ignites me again." You feel that you're a natural teacher. It's always come easily to you, and you've always been ready and willing to roll with the punches. But boredom has been creeping up on your career.

What Burnout Stage Are You?

Now that you know your burnout type, let's set you up on a path to success. Look at the following stage descriptions (0 to 5), and you'll find the Teacher Success Roadmap to becoming a BURNED-IN teacher. This will help you identify what stage of burnout you're in, no matter what type you are, and the milestones you'll likely encounter along the way.

Take a few minutes to read all of the stages. As you look through this Success Roadmap, look for things you feel, do, and think about regularly. When you find a stage that most closely matches your current reality, circle or highlight it. Remember, it doesn't have to be spot-on, but rather a place you can relate to at this point in time. Identifying yourself with a stage will allow you to track milestones and seek growth as we go on this journey.

The Six Stages on the Teacher Success Roadmap:

Stage 0

Stage 1

Stage 2

Stage 3

Stage 4

Stage 5

Stage 0:

Stage 0 is tricky, because chances are, as you've already engaged with this book, you've moved out of this stage. Stage 0 is easy to identify in other people, and you may recognize it in your past self before you decided to take action, like reading this book.

When you're in Stage 0, you see no point in doing anything: getting out of bed, talking to your friends, or even going to work. You're so ashamed, sad, and isolated in this place of burnout that you don't know where to start or even if you can make changes. You may have convinced yourself that this is "just the way it is" and that this is it for you.

All you can think about is how horrible your life is, how much you hate your job or the people there, and how you know that you can't tell anyone, because they won't understand.

Stage 1:

In this stage, you've admitted that you're feeling burnout, but you haven't changed your beliefs surrounding your feelings and thoughts every day. Negativity and guilt consume you, and you blame yourself and others for where you are in your career. Your self-talk and outward conversations reflect your feelings of victimization, and you know the only option is to quit your job and do something different.

You dread every morning and wonder how you even got to this place in your life and career. You may find yourself asking, "What am I even doing here?"

Stage 2:

In this stage, your thinking begins to change from "Why is this happening to me?" to "What can I do about it?" Your validation and curiosity are leading you down a path to search for answers and support. You're opening conversations about how you're feeling and also asking questions that are moving you forward.

As you reflect on what's challenging you, you're also thinking about what you used to love about teaching, what you miss, and how to bring more of that back into your daily teaching life.

Stage 3:

Stage 3 is a game-changer. This is where you begin to feel activated and proactive. You've identified your triggers, challenges, and strengths. You're thinking about what you want for yourself, and not just as a teacher. You're looking at what brings you joy, and you're willing to make the changes necessary to see positive results.

You may even find yourself taking risks and doing things you've never done in order to move further and faster out of burnout. This is a transformational stage.

Stage 4:

Now you're on fire. Because you're setting goals that truly mean something to you, and you have a healthy system of support around you, you're able to be intentional about making progress every day. You continually find yourself inspired by those around you, and your plan of action evolves as you bring more people into your life who want what you want: a happier and more fulfilled life.

You are closer to reaching your goals each day, and you're planning for if and when "life happens" and hardship arises. Even in uncertain times, your blinders are on, and you continue to be engaged in your daily life.

Stage 5:

When you're at Stage 5, you feel empowered to make solid decisions about what you do and do not commit to, and you are as close to balanced as you can be most days. You look at your daily plan with flexibility and know that even when things don't go the way you want, you are organized enough to get back on track. You're sleeping better than ever and rewriting your story as a journey that you are grateful for, because you wouldn't be able to be the person you are today without it. Yes, you heard me right. You're grateful for the burnout.

You wake up most days with a sense of passion and a renewed strength that you once thought you would never possess.

For more details about learning your Teacher Burnout Type and Stage, see the BURNED-IN Teacher Resources section in the back of this book.

Now that you know your type and stage, you're on your journey out of burnout. Consider these two pieces of information as important as the first items you pack when going on a trip. You will use your burnout type and stage to assess your growth throughout these Hacks. This journey has started with you deciding that you will no longer settle for negativity, doubt, hopelessness, exhaustion, and victimization. You won't settle for a life you don't control or that you try to escape from. Good for you!

As you finish each Hack, you'll have the opportunity to measure your progress out of burnout as you reflect, implement, and continue your journey. Each step is easy to read, but your actions will depend on you, your reality, and your goals.

Completing the A Blueprint for Full Implementation within each Hack will allow you to interact with the content, your situation, and your feelings and take professional and personal action to triumph over your biggest challenges. I encourage you to use a notebook to record your reflections and revisit them regularly. This practice will enable you to reduce your likelihood of burnout in the future because when challenges arise, you always will have this eight-step process to give you clarity and focus.

Now, you're ready. Let's Hack Teacher Burnout!

HACK 1

B: BEGIN WHERE YOU ARE
REFLECT ON WHAT BROUGHT YOU
TO WHERE YOU ARE NOW

The past is a place of reference, not a place of residence.
— ROY T. BENNETT, AUTHOR

THE PROBLEM: YOU'RE BURNED-OUT, STUCK, AND ASHAMED

I'T'S HARD TO assess your current reality and how it came to be when you're just trying to keep your head above water. As teachers, we often don't allow ourselves the time to reflect on where we started, where we are, how we got here, and where we want to be. Teaching creates a feeling of blurriness with thousands of decisions, details, and responsibilities every day that cloud our minds. And that blurriness keeps us from seeing our situation—and our burnout—clearly.

When you Google "burnout," you are met with a range of symptoms:

- Energy depletion or exhaustion

- Increased mental distance from your job
- Feelings of negativity or cynicism related to teaching
- Reduced professional efficacy

You may recognize those signs from the introduction, and as you reread them, you've probably already identified with most of them. Then you may stop because although you recognize the signs and symptoms, you think you don't have time to move forward.

With all we have to do as teachers every day, we sometimes slip into survival mode. And "surviving" the day has become a common statement in our classrooms and schools. When you're merely surviving, you don't have the mindset or energy to think about what you might be doing instead. You don't have the time or energy to think about being proactive. Proactivity takes time, thought, and planning, and our brains are hardwired to do the safest and most conservative thing when faced with a hardship or a challenging decision.

BY ASSESSING WHY YOU ARE WHERE YOU ARE, YOU WILL GET TO THE HOW OF MOVING FORWARD ON YOUR JOURNEY OUT OF BURNOUT.

That means we often take the easier path when given a choice between two options. For instance, when we're at a crossroads between A) complaining about a hardship and settling for things the way they are, or B) actively doing something different to change our situation, our brains typically tell us to complain and continue business as usual because it burns fewer calories (a survival mechanism from our ancestors).

When you're burned-out and stuck, those sorts of decisions are the ones that keep you stuck as the days, weeks, months, and years roll on. We find ourselves on the perpetual "burnout roller coaster," full of highs and lows, twists and turns, and all the anxiety and fear that come with sitting in that cart as the ride begins.

When you say, "I'm burned-out" and do nothing about it, you adopt the belief that the following statements are true and abundant:

- "I don't know what I want."
- "I know what I want, but it won't work."
- "I'm alone, and no one else knows how this feels."
- "I'm stuck here."
- "I'm just a statistic."
- "Everyone is judging me."
- "My only option is to quit."
- "I can't talk about it."
- "If I wait long enough, someone will have an answer for me, or someone will save me."

The problem with these statements is that they breed helplessness and victimization. They take away your power and make you feel like you have no voice or choice in what your future holds or no responsibility for your life—in or out of the classroom.

But you're not choosing the victim's path or mentality now, or ever again. No, you're going to be proactive and focus on taking back your power. You're ready to take responsibility, action, and initiative, so let's dive into some Hacks to get you started on your journey out of burnout.

THE HACK: BEGIN WHERE YOU ARE

It's time to change the conversation surrounding burnout. To do this, you must give your burnout the respect, time, and reflection it deserves so you can figure out how you got to where you are in the first place. Let's look at burnout as a desire for growth and change, and act on those desires before it's too late. You can start by asking the following questions:

- How long have I been teaching?

- When did I start feeling frustrated, out of balance, bored, anxious, unappreciated, apathetic, ashamed, or isolated?

- What caused those feelings to arise?

- Did I acknowledge them when they first started showing up? If not, why?

- What changed in my life that could have caused the start of my burnout?

- What have I already tried to do to solve my feelings of burnout?

- Who knows about the struggles I'm having?

After you address the what and why that brought you to this place, you can start believing that there is a reason you're reading this book. You know where you are … but do you know where you want to go? Trust the process as you move from here to there, and know that you're doing the right thing for yourself.

It all starts with beginning where you are, and that has every-thing to do with reflecting and reassessing your past—and nothing to do with regret. You're seeking to understand your current reality. Period.

By assessing *why* you are where you are, you will get to the *how* of moving forward on your journey out of burnout.

WHAT YOU CAN DO TOMORROW

There is power in the courage it takes to be vulnerable enough to admit that you're struggling or needing help. So say it right now, wherever you are: "I'm burned-out." Good for you. That's part of Step 1. And that's where a lot of people in burnout stop and stay. But you? You're going to take action. You're going to learn about you and your burnout, and when you educate yourself, you're empowering yourself to think, feel, believe, and do differently than you ever have before. Get started with understanding how you got here in the first place by taking the following simple actions:

- **Take the Teacher Burnout Quiz.** Find the quiz at burnedinteacher.com/burnoutquiz, and get to know your burnout better by answering six simple questions about where you are and how you feel about your current reality in your job. It's quick and offers insight into your burnout like you never knew was possible.

- **Brainstorm a list of people who could become your "Burnout Buddies."** These are people who can support you through your journey out of burnout. You're going to need someone to help you through the hard days and someone to celebrate wins with you. And you need to decide who they are now. Share all aspects of your current reality with them, including the results from your quiz, questionnaire, and your journey starting here in Hack 1. If you don't have anyone in your direct personal or professional life you feel you can trust, then develop a Professional Learning Network (PLN) through social media.

- **List your top stressors at home.** Chances are, personal struggles or changes are impacting your overall reality. List all answers to these two questions:

  1. What's happening in my personal life that could be impacting my happiness and fulfillment at work?

  2. What personal, family, social, and global changes have occurred that could be affecting my mood, beliefs, and overall attitude?

- **Research core values.** What two words will help ground you when you're deciding to say "yes" or "no" to something? These are words you'll come back to when you're struggling with your purpose, and these words will help you connect to your people (including those you serve).

- **Decide who you want to serve the most.** In the business world, your people are your customers. You work for them, even though they don't sign your paychecks. In education, your people are those for whom you do all of this incredibly hard work and strive to impact the most every day. They are your *why* for being in education in the first place.

A BLUEPRINT FOR FULL IMPLEMENTATION

Deciding to admit that you're burned-out and then doing something about it takes work. You must take intentional action from here on out to see growth out of your particular type of burnout. Are you ready to get to work? Follow these four steps, and you'll be on your way to leaving the burnout behind.

STEP 1: Identify your burnout type and stage of burnout.

If you skipped the part of the Introduction where I gave you a condensed version of the three different Burnout Types and Stages of Burnout, go there now to identify what type you're dealing with and how burned-out you are.

Teachers experience three types of burnout: Burned and Over

It, Burned and Unbalanced, or Burned and Bored. You can encounter them at any point in your career, perhaps more than once, and not in any particular order. Imagine the three types as different reasons that you would visit a doctor. They're all reasons for concern, but one is a broken foot, one is a high fever and cough, and the other is debilitating back pain—all serious, yet all needing a different treatment.

Now, we need to identify *your* stage of burnout. It provides a benchmark to continually check in on your progress as you make your way through the Hacks in this book and take action to go from burned-out to BURNED-IN. Knowing that right now you're at Stage 1 or 2, for example, is helpful, because as you move through the Hacks, you'll be able to assess what you're thinking, feeling, and doing, and how much you've grown from where you started.

It's impossible to know how far you have to go unless you know where you're starting.

STEP 2: Identify your burnout triggers.

It's time for you to travel back in time. Yes, I know. People may have told you to leave the past in the past, and that's good advice. However, burnout is called burnout for a reason. It isn't a bolt of lightning from a blue sky or even from a storm cloud. That's too predictable and immediate.

Burnout usually stems from a slow burn, which creeps up on you as you move through your daily life. It's barely noticeable. You shove it to the side—until it begins to consume everything about teaching that you once loved. Burnout is tricky, and for this reason, often hard to beat. But you can do it.

When I reflect on my struggle with teacher burnout (I managed to suffer from all three types of burnout at different points in my career), I notice many triggers that contributed to my downward spiral into burnout. While teaching, I ignored those signs, symptoms, blaring issues, sirens, and even an apocalypse that was happening inside of me. The zombies on the inside finally caused me to have emotional breakdowns, and I even ignored those. Can you believe it? That was no way to live. I mean, ignorance is bliss, but I was far from blissful. I was depressed, moody, isolated, and aggressive. For the sake of what? Was I afraid of appearing weak?

At that point, I showed my weakness in a big way by breaking down publicly in front of my coworkers multiple times, just ten minutes before working with students. I even reenacted this scenario twice.

The strange thing was, I loved teaching while all this was happening. Cue another left hook from burnout. I often asked myself these questions and told myself these lies:

- How can you be so ungrateful?

- What's wrong with you?

- You're worthless. You have all of this in front of you, and you're throwing it all away.

- You'll never be enough.

- You're too stupid to grow into a leadership position.

I said all these things instead of paying attention to patterns, triggers, and changes happening around me and leading me down this burnout path.

Here's what I *should* have asked myself:

- How long have I physically been here?
  - How long have I been in this school district?
  - How long have I been in this building, grade level, or physical classroom?
- Have any changes started this slow burn?
- Have any changes in my life affected my mental or emotional state?
- How long have I mentally/emotionally been here?
  - How long have I felt frustrated, disengaged, isolated, or anxious?
- Have I tried anything new since these feelings arose?
- Have I talked to anyone and asked for support, advice, or mentorship?

Now it's your turn.

Take a deep breath and close your eyes. Think about your patterns, triggers, and changes. Your mind may summon to the surface thoughts you continually revisit and thoughts you've kept pushed down for a while. Either way, those thoughts are asking for your attention. Maybe they're demanding it. If you feel moved to get these thoughts into the open air, take time to jot them down or say them out loud. We'll come back to this.

Knowing your burnout type, stage, and the events leading up to them are essential components to tackling burnout, because knowing the what, where, and how of your burnout will allow you to have more activated conversations about it.

STEP 3: Identify your people.

An important part of identifying the people you want to serve is to realize that they are your thermometer. When you decide on your career, you're going to ask yourself, "Is this thought, action, or conversation moving the needle forward for those I serve? Is it helping me serve them? Or is it taking my energy away from serving them?"

I simply define your people (when it comes to your professional life) as those who you want to impact the most as an educator. Although it's crucial to build relationships in some way with everyone you work with, your people are those you serve the most, those for whom you're doing this work. They give you purpose and are the why behind all your hard work.

Your people could be your students, their families, your administrator(s), or colleagues. You also could include yourself in this list, especially if you realize you've been neglecting your own life and need to prioritize your time.

Focusing your efforts on your people will help you create a healthier, more positive mindset around what you can and cannot control as you move through your burnout.

STEP 4: Identify your core values.

Core values are words that sum up your fundamental beliefs. They help you determine if you're on the right path or not. They are guiding principles when you're making tough decisions, and they represent your highest priorities. A Google search for a list of core value words will bring up many resources to check out as you decide what values you want to guide you through this and other life journeys.

Core values will help you determine what some people call "your truth." Living your truth means living in a way that is best for you, fully embracing yourself as a person, and honoring your values and goals. We'll start slowly with core values and build on these as you continue through the Hacks.

Some experts say you should have one focused value. Yet others, like Brené Brown in *Dare to Lead*, say you should have two. I'm not going to tell you what is best for you. You can determine this for yourself. As you research words that you believe reflect your truth, narrow them down to five or fewer. Beyond five, you may start to overlap words and meanings and make this task more difficult than it needs to be.

I've currently resolved to choose two—empowerment and compassion—and be flexible with my values as I reach milestones. Empowerment and compassion are my *current* values because these are words that people have used to describe me for a long time (in fact, it's part of my brand, which we'll talk about in the next Hack).

Your core values will guide you as you decide what practices and habits to abandon, adjust, or adopt to serve your people.

OVERCOMING PUSHBACK

What's hard about the following pushback examples is that they may be pushback from *you*. And unfortunately, you may also hear these things from your fellow teachers or influencers on social media. Misery loves company, and your self-talk loves to keep you stuck (more on this in Hack 2), but you don't have to succumb to the negativity that is so popular and prevalent in your head and IG feed.

There's so much to do; I don't have time to do any of this. As you'll learn in Hack 2, what you choose to believe will be your reality. So if you choose to believe that you aren't worthy of taking the time to move through these steps and put them into action, then that will be your truth. However, I encourage you to believe that you are capable and worthy of the time it will take to reflect, act upon, and grow because of this book. It will take time, but the momentum you will build by taking small steps each day will be worth your effort. I promise.

This is just the way it is. Of course, it is the way it is. You're looking around and either thinking or hearing, "Well, this is a hot mess, and it will always be a hot mess." But this is why Hack 1 is called Begin Where You Are. When you hear this statement in your head, or if someone says it to you, it's okay to look around and reply, "You're right. This is the way it is, but I choose not to stay stuck in these feelings, beliefs, and the 'norm' of burnout."

There is power in knowing that some things are the way they are when it comes to policies, families, and school norms. But acknowledging the reality and accepting it moves you into radical acceptance, which is a Buddhist belief. According to psychologist Marsha Linehan, when you practice radical acceptance, you "rest on letting go of the illusion of control and a willingness to notice and accept things the way they are right now without judging" (we'll talk more about this in Hack 3).

I'm a bad teacher for feeling burned-out. Someone may make you feel this way, whether it's coming from your self-talk or from the whispers of teachers down the hall, who are throwing you shade instead of a life vest as they watch you drown. Either way, know that you are a good teacher for wanting different or better circumstances for yourself. This is your one life, after all.

It's okay if you don't love putting in sixty-plus hours of work a week, learning all the new technology, and tackling students' personal and home challenges on an hourly basis. It's okay to want to work in a place and in a way that you feel energized and joyful. It's not selfish to live your truth. You deserve it.

Your burnout comes from a call for growth or change, and the more you ignore it, the more you're going to feel it. Beginning where you are is all about knowing where you are, so you have the clarity to see where you want to go. And that's okay.

Once you're burned-out, there's no coming back. Although burnout will change you, the change can be positive if you choose to take careful action when you know what your burnout type is and what stage you're in. There's truth in the saying, "What doesn't get measured, doesn't get managed." And by knowing your burnout type and stage, you've measured where you are. Now you can manage your burnout.

This pushback statement is twofold. You have the potential to move from your current reality and never return, and that's a good thing.

You also have the potential to never return to this type of burnout, though you could feel a different type of burnout creep up in the future. The difference is that you're going to equip yourself with the steps and strategies you'll need to Never Settle (Hack 8) for accepting that burnout means you're terrible, selfish, stuck, or "done" in education. Because it certainly does not.

THE HACK IN ACTION
By Sarah K., middle school ELA teacher

Now that I think back, I can't recall a point in my past teaching career when I didn't feel "burned-out." I even took a year off from teaching after completing my student teaching because I was concerned that my life was destined to become that of my cooperating teachers: exhausting, stressed, and empty of time for family or friends outside of school. I didn't want a life like that, so I left teaching. But a year of working at a bank reinvigorated that feeling deep down that I was meant to be a teacher. So I made a choice and went back into the classroom, feeling positive that I wouldn't let my job control my life.

My first teaching job was exactly what I left teaching to avoid: it was stressful, overwhelming, and made up of ridiculous time commitments. As a first-year teacher, I taught eighth grade English and sixth grade accelerated math, and I was the ESL coordinator for the district, the AP coordinator in the high school, and the gifted and talented coordinator for the middle school and high school. I was one of the student council advisors, and I had an hour commute twice a day. I was exhausted, but I told myself the lie that many teachers tell themselves: I need to do all the things to be a good teacher. I had decided to go back to teaching, and I knew, deep down, that this was where I was meant to be. So I accepted this as my reality, because one, I didn't know better, and two, this was the story that I had been told while in college.

Then, something big happened: I became pregnant with my first child. Becoming pregnant put life in perspective for me. I didn't want my job to take control of my life; I wanted to be the best mommy I could be. So I worked hard to find a teaching job closer to home and without all the responsibilities. I was successful in this endeavor, and I thought all my problems were solved.

While I no longer had all the many responsibilities, I was still spending most of my time at school and taking work home. Even with a new baby at home, I worked several hours a night and never seemed to get ahead. I talked with my mentor and other teachers that I worked with about my challenges, and they reiterated what I was told in college: you will always have tons to do and not enough time to do it. Their suggestion was to bring my kids with me on a Saturday and let them play while I did work, or come in on a Sunday to work before my family woke up. To these teachers, their suggestions seemed logical because that was what they did. They gave more of themselves and sacrificed their time. I never took this advice, but my workload and lack of fulfillment never changed. As I continued down that path, I got to a bad place. I never hung out with friends or even talked with them anymore, and I hardly ever hung out with my husband. I didn't take the time to take care of myself, and I gave up so much of what made me "me." *But it is all part of the job*, I would tell myself over and over while I watched my life speed by.

But I wanted something different. I felt guilty for feeling unfulfilled and unhappy, and I stuffed all those feelings down and continued to tell myself that this was part of the job. But I knew deep down that this was not okay, that I was not okay. So I accepted that something was not right with my reality and sought the help that I needed to move forward with the life I wanted and knew I deserved. At that moment, I accepted my current reality for what it was and began my journey out of burnout. It was a process, and I needed to work at it daily. But none of this growth would have been possible if I did not accept my reality for what it was and use that momentum to make life-altering changes.

For you to move out of burnout, you must do things you've never done before, such as naming your burnout and identifying your burnout stage. These steps may seem silly and unconventional, but they are critical when it comes to accepting your burnout, respecting it by identifying your triggers, and then allowing yourself to think about your purpose and who your people are.

Showing vulnerability, admitting you're struggling, and seeking support aren't signs of weakness. On the contrary, it takes a lot of courage to look at your current reality and realize that you need to change it. Once you do that, you can move to Hack 2 and build self-awareness with a clear understanding of *how* you got to where you are—and how to get out of it.

HACK 2

U: UNDERSTAND YOUR TEACHER BRAND
AWAKEN YOUR SELF-AWARENESS AND BUILD A TEACHER BRAND YOU CAN BE PROUD OF

Your beliefs become your thoughts, your thoughts become your words, your words become your actions, your actions become your habits, your habits become your values, your values become your destiny.

— MAHATMA GANDHI, LAWYER AND ETHICIST

THE PROBLEM: YOU'VE LOST TOUCH WITH WHO YOU ARE AND WHY YOU DO WHAT YOU DO

NOW THAT YOU know your burnout type, stage, triggers, people, and core values, we will build your self-awareness and get you further along your path out of burnout.

Having strong self-awareness is essential to beating burnout because if you don't know who you are, it's impossible to get your feet under you and figure out how to go forward. And although you used to have a reason for teaching, burnout has turned your identity into a pile of ashes. Your burnout type and stage have taken over what used to be you. Perhaps your burnout has taken away your purpose, and you no longer do what you love to do or dream about doing in the future, like coaching or being a dad.

Just as it's hard to pay attention to your reality when you're trying to keep your head above water, it's hard to focus on yourself and what you think, believe, say, and do on a daily basis when you're burned-out. When you lose your self-awareness, you lose the ability to remember why you're even doing what you're doing anymore, and you become numb to your everyday actions—from what you eat for breakfast to how you reply to students when they talk to you in class.

Have you ever had a student or one of your own children say something to you, and you reply with, "That's nice. Way to go." When you look up, they're staring at you as if you just spoke a different language, and they say, "What do you think I just said?"

What happens when you lose touch with your self-awareness and stop thinking about your everyday beliefs, habits, and routines? You simply go through the motions. I compare it to Bernie from the '90s classic *Weekend at Bernie's*. In the movie, Bernie dies unexpectedly, but his renters decide to pretend that he's alive, making it seem that he's just going about his day doing all of his usual activities: taking walks on the beach, making cocktails by the pool while listening to his favorite music, having dinner with friends—all the things that made Bernie, Bernie.

But he's dead. He's going through the motions without feeling a thing.

When you feel like you're just going through the motions, you live on autopilot. And although it's good to have habits and routines, the routine you've fallen into doesn't serve you or your purpose anymore. Depending on your burnout type, you've fallen into beliefs that affect what you think, say, and do each day.

The most dangerous part is that you don't even know how bad it's gotten. Your burnout has caused you to ditch your old beliefs about why you're doing what you do every day and who you are, and put you into a perpetual state of one of these two beliefs:

- I can control everything. If it looks like I've got it all together, then I will have it all together.

- Nothing I do matters. It doesn't matter what I do or say, how my classroom appears, or whether I show up to work.

The danger here is that you've now thrown a coat of paint on an empty building to try to justify your numbness. You say things like, "I'm just a control freak" or "I just go with the flow," and you've created a false sense of self: "I am who I am, and no one understands that except for me."

The only way to get back to who you truly are is to re-engage with yourself and build or rebuild your teacher brand.

THE HACK: UNDERSTAND YOUR TEACHER BRAND

Thanks to the work you did in Hack 1, you can increase your self-awareness when it comes to your teacher brand. With the help of your students, colleagues, and administrators, you can build or rebuild a brand you can be proud to represent.

If you're confused about what your brand is or how to build one, don't worry. That's what this Hack is all about. It's fairly simple to find out your current brand because your brand is whatever your people say it is. It's the cross-section where your core values and purpose match what your people see as your core values and purpose, based on your words, actions, and care for yourself, your things, and your content.

Branding yourself means consistently behaving, speaking, and living in a way that creates a certain perception about who you are and what you can do. People in your realm of influence, including your students, their families, your colleagues, superiors, and your learning community, will come to expect a level of personality and professionalism based on the teacher brand you live.

BY THE END OF THIS HACK, YOU'LL HAVE THE TOOLS YOU NEED TO FIND YOURSELF AGAIN AND RE-CREATE A BRAND THAT WILL AWAKEN YOU FROM YOUR BURNOUT SLUMBER.

You never know who is paying attention, either. There may be a teacher down the hall from you who will become a principal at a school in the next district where you want to work. They'll form their opinion of you based on the brand you build, and that brand might alter their willingness to work with you in the future. Bottom line: your teacher brand matters.

If you're unhappy with your current brand, you can improve it or change it altogether. You can rebrand yourself. Yes! Just like Target did in the early 2000s. Just like Miley Cyrus has done many times. Remember Hannah Montana in 2006? Now think of how different Miley's brand was in 2013 compared to her sitcom days. She's rebranded herself many times over by the way she acts, what she says, and the people she hangs out with the most.

It's important to understand that brands are different than judgments, and this Hack isn't about keeping up with the "education Joneses" or becoming the most popular teacher in the school or on Instagram. It isn't about creating the next viral video or becoming TikTok famous. It's about having a good character and making sure it shines through your beliefs, actions, and words.

Judgment = an opinion created based on a chance encounter.

Brands are based on repeated patterns of interactions people have had with you over time, whether in person or virtually. Yes, even the way you conduct yourself online is part of your brand. If people who know you well can predict what you're going to say or how you're going to react to certain situations or settings before you say or do anything, you have defined your brand.

To help you determine how others (especially your people) perceive you, let me ask you a few gut-check questions:

- When you turn the corner in your school and happen upon a group of people talking, how do they react to your presence?

- Before a school meeting or collaboration, who sits by you, or who do you sit near?

- If you were other teachers, what would you say about you?

- If you were to ask your students what they thought about you, what would they say?

- Consider your last meeting with your administrator. What was it about? How did you feel when you left the meeting?

- Think about parent interactions you've had both inside and outside of school. What was the demeanor of the parent(s) toward you?

By the end of this Hack, you'll have the tools you need to find yourself again and re-create a brand that will awaken you from your burnout slumber.

Like in Hack 1, where you dug around in the outside forces of your past and current reality, we must dig around inwardly to figure out what has been happening to create your (now autopilot) beliefs, actions, habits, and ongoing routine.

Doing this is simple, but your findings may be hard to accept. As you start to wake from this perpetual, eyes-wide-open slumber, you realize that the brand you may have built for yourself is causing a ripple effect of negative relationships, piles of work, or boredom—depending, of course, on your burnout type.

WHAT YOU CAN DO TOMORROW

Understanding your teacher brand doesn't have to be hard, but it does have to be intentional for you to move to the next (improved) burnout stage. Be honest with yourself about what you perceive about your brand versus what others perceive about it. Building self-awareness can be hard, but enlightening. You can build better self-awareness and move through the burnout stages by paying attention to your five senses. Imagine you're waking up, stretching, and taking in your everyday environment for the first time. Use your senses to "wake up" and observe the brand you've created for yourself.

- **Look.** Pay attention to:
    - Your classroom or workspace. Imagine you're looking at this space for the first time. How does it make you feel?
    - How you present yourself. Check out your reflection in the mirror. Do you appear to be ready to serve your people?
    - Your home and car. As you walk into your home or get into your car, imagine that your teacher friends are with you. What do your home and car say about your brand?
    - Your social media account. If a student, parent, or future principal landed on your social media accounts, what would your accounts say about you?

- **Listen.** Pay attention to the conversations you have:
    - In your head
    - With colleagues and administrators
    - With students in your classroom
    - In the hallways

What do you hear? What stands out to you? Take a mental note or use a notebook to track what words or phrases you hear yourself or your colleagues say the most.

- **Smell.** Pay attention as you "sniff" around other teachers' brands by taking a walk through your school or thinking about each classroom as you take that walk mentally. Maybe it's been a while since you've intentionally left your hallway. If so, this is an even more perfect time to "sniff around."
    - How do you feel as you walk by other rooms?
    - What do other teachers' classrooms say about them?
    - What words do they use?
    - How do they present themselves regularly?

Using voice memos or a notebook to reflect, answer these questions as you walk around the school. This may be better done before or after school when fewer teachers are around to wonder what you're up to.

- **Touch.** Pay attention as you "reach out and touch someone you trust," and ask them:
    - "What words would you use to describe me? Please be honest; I'm working on my brand." (To which they may say … "What's a brand? I want one!")
    - "When you hear students, other teachers, and our principal talk about my class and me, what do they say? Lay it on me; I can take it."
    - "Would you want your student in my class? Why or why not?"

Record their answers or record the conversation—with the teacher's permission, of course. You might hear things differently than you ever have before, simply because you're waking up your senses and building your self-awareness.

- **Taste.** Get a "taste" of what your students and colleagues feel about your brand. Pay attention to reactions when you give your students a "taste" of a different teacher brand than the one you may be projecting, and when you ask for their interpretation of you.

  - Do or say something that you wouldn't normally do or say (within reason, of course), and observe their reactions. How do they look at you? What do they say?

  - Ask your students for their opinions about you as a teacher and their opinions about your class. "What do you enjoy most about this class?" "How well do you feel you know me?" "If you could change something about this class, what would it be?" "What would you tell a new student about our classroom and me?"

  - Write down all the words that you'd *like* people to use to describe you. And go deeper than the surface. What type of person would you want your people to say you are?

  - Now it's time for action research. Go out into the field and see what your people are saying. You can create a Google Form or free survey on SurveyMonkey to simply ask the question: "When you think about me or hear my name, what words come to mind?" Give them choices, if you'd like, based on what you think you may hear. Or leave it open-ended. It's up to you. Does your initial list align with what your people say? What adjectives are similar? Different?

Now that you've collected these observations using your five senses, you can sit with them and look for trends. Sit with your burnout buddy and go over your results. Talking this out, gaining a different perspective, and reflecting on what you've noticed will help you as you build or rebuild a brand that aligns better with your values and purpose. Find yourself again, and you'll start to find a way to climb out of the burnout you've been feeling.

A BLUEPRINT FOR FULL IMPLEMENTATION

When I began to take serious action against my burnout in 2014, I read the book *Awaken the Giant Within* by Tony Robbins. He wrote, "Simply by changing your habitual vocabulary—the words you consistently use to describe the emotions in your life—you can instantaneously change how you think, how you feel, and how you live." I didn't know it then, but what Tony is talking about is the development of a personal brand. Using your research with your five senses and talking it out with someone you trust will help you put your findings to work. The following steps will help you refine that process in the long term.

STEP 1: Understand your mission statement.

In Hack 1, you decided to focus on two core values. Say them out loud. (If you forgot, then you still don't know them in your core and should likely reconsider whether the ones you chose are relevant enough.)

As we discussed, your core values are a vital component to helping you establish your teacher brand. They are necessary to create your personal mission statement. Here's the simplest way I can put this:

Your professional mission statement defines your teacher brand. Literally, it is *who* you serve (your people), *what* you do to serve them, *how* you serve them, and *why*. Additionally, I believe that your mission statement should include your two core values. Here's a sentence stem for you:

I value_____and_____. I help _____ understand/do _____ so that _____.

Examples:

> "I create **confident** leaders in my students by teaching them ways to think for themselves, make decisions with independence, and choose **kindness**, because their future depends on it." (A kindergarten teacher's mission statement.)

> "I activate teacher **self-empowerment** by showing **compassion** to educators struggling with teacher burnout and empowering them with the action, inspiration, and support they need to take the next best steps in their careers and in life." (That's mine.)

The bold words? Those are core values. Inject them into your mission statement like you're injecting marinade in a turkey. Really get them up in there.

Now look at your mission statement and look at yourself in the mirror. Then take a look around your classroom. Does the way you're presenting yourself show your mission statement?

Yourself:

- Do you appear well-rested or exhausted?

- Does the look on your face consistently project positivity or negativity?

Your places:

- Are you well-organized? Is your desk tidy? Is your classroom neat? Or are you always hunting through piles of papers strewn about or changing the schedule because you can't find the day's original plans or materials?

- Or are you so organized that you've become a "Label Dictator," where everything has to be perfect, color-coded, and #Pinterestworthy, and you always stress about it?

Considering your presentation of yourself and your classroom in this way isn't about vanity or making it look like you've got it all together. It's not about breaking the bank on a completely new wardrobe and blaming the credit card bill on Amber. Creating your teacher brand isn't about changing who you *are*; it's about making sure your beliefs, actions, and words align with your people, values, and purpose for doing what you do. A brand is about how you view yourself and how you project your self-worth to the world. Having the right brand empowers you.

Having the wrong brand adds to burnout because you're not presenting your true self to the world.

I also encourage you to take this practice one step further. Notice that this is all about your professional mission statement and teacher brand, yet you also have a life outside of school. Consider creating a mission statement that encompasses your whole life.

STEP 2: Change your beliefs and self-talk.

Buddha said, "What you think, you become. What you feel, you attract. What you imagine, you create."

This internal belief system is especially important to note before you can begin to make significant changes in your life. As you reflect on what brought you to this place in your career, realize that those factors had to do with outside influences that caused you to feel dread, anxiety, and frustration at some point in your career.

However, we haven't addressed what has been going on inside of your mind for the past weeks, months, and even years as you created the thought habits that drag you further down the path of burnout.

Identifying your self-talk habits and changing the way you talk to yourself will hugely impact whether you make your way out of burnout. We must start deep inside your head, break the bad habits, and get your mind right so you can get your life right.

As author and psychiatrist Dan Siegel said, "If you can name it, you can tame it." By now, you know that giving things a name is extremely important to this whole idea and process, and we're going to name something else: the voices in your head that are keeping you the same and those that will help you create change in your life.

AGENTS OF SAME	AGENTS OF CHANGE
PERFECTION PATTY "If this isn't perfect, it isn't good enough to use or do." Feelings: doubt, uncertainty	**TRY-IT-OUT TREVOR** "I am brave enough to try new things, make mistakes, and learn from them." Feelings: confident, inspired
OVERWHELM OLIVIA "There's so much to do, I don't know where to start!" Feelings: panic, stress	**STEP-BY-STEP SABRINA** "I will focus on what will have the biggest impact on my VISION." Feelings: focused, organized
NEGATIVE NED "Shocker. This always happens to me." Feelings: exasperated, frustrated	**POSITIVITY PEYTON** "I can do hard things, and I won't let challenges affect my attitude." Feelings: grateful, calm
ANXIOUS AVERY "What if …?" Feelings: scarcity, irritated	**GO-WITH-THE-FLOW FRANK** "I am not going to worry about things I can't control." Feelings: clarity, thoughtful
SUPERHERO SAM "I can do everything myself." Feelings: isolated, overwhelmed	**HUMAN HANNAH** "I am going to focus on what I can do, with the time I am allowed and will ask for help, when I need it." Feelings: relieved, determined
EXCUSE EDWARD "I'm too … (insert belief here)." Feelings: inferior, incapable	**CAPABLE CARRIE** "I am capable, and I am worthy." Feelings: capable, worthy

Image 2.1: Use this chart to help you identify the Agents of Change that replace the Agents of Same. For more details, see the BURNED-IN Resources section in the back.

Enter the Self-Talk Agents. When you can name the Self-Salk Agent you're dealing with, it's easier to identify it as an Agent of Same (keeping you in that place of sameness) or an Agent of Change (helping you move forward toward your goals and empowering you to make necessary changes). See Image 2.1.

My Agents of Same even have individual names that reflect the feelings they evoke when I call on them. Here are their names and what you may hear them say:

Perfection Patty says, "If this isn't perfect, it isn't good enough to use or do." That creates feelings of doubt and uncertainty.

Overwhelm Olivia says, "There's so much to do; I don't know where to start." That creates feelings of panic and stress.

Negative Ned says, "Shocker. This always happens to me" or "Of course ... this is always what happens." That creates feelings of exasperation and frustration.

Anxious Avery says, "What if ... " and ends each of these with a negative outcome, creating feelings of irritation and scarcity.

Superhero Sam says, "I can do everything myself." That creates feelings of isolation and overwhelm.

Excuse Edward says, "I'm too ... " and ends this sentence with any number of excuses for why one can't or won't make changes to their current reality.

Do you see? All of these Agents of Same keep you where you are: stuck, negative, overwhelmed, or ashamed. And that's the vital point about your self-talk and what it can mean for your destiny if you continue to allow these statements to infiltrate your mind daily.

Did you know that, according to the National Science Foundation, 80 percent of our daily thoughts are negative? A whole

80 percent. And in addition to that, 95 percent of our thoughts today are repeated thoughts from yesterday.

Think about that for a second. If you were wondering at the beginning of this section why we need to learn about and identify your self-talk habits, now you have your answer. You cannot make any changes or take any of the actions suggested in this book unless you change first—starting with your self-talk habits.

To help you with that and assist you in kicking these nasty Agents of Same to the burnout curb, I'd like to introduce you to the Agents of Change.

The Agents of Change are voices that will help you combat the Agents of Same and change your self-talk and your actions. As I mentioned at the beginning of this section, "What you think, you become."

So, here are the Agents of Change and what they say:

Try-It-Out Trever says, "I am brave enough to try new things, make mistakes, and learn from them." That creates feelings of confidence and inspiration.

Step-by-Step Sabrina says, "I will focus on what will have the biggest impact on my vision." That creates feelings of focus and organization.

Positivity Peyton says, "I can do hard things, and I won't let challenges affect my attitude." That creates feelings of gratitude and calm.

Go-with-the-Flow Frank says, "I am not going to worry about things I can't control." That creates feelings of clarity and thoughtfulness.

Human Hannah says, "I am going to focus on what I can do with the time I am allowed and will ask for help when I need it." That creates feelings of relief and determination.

Capable Carrie says, "I am capable, and I am worthy." That creates feelings of capability and worthiness.

Many teachers and administrators have found these named self-talk agents to be the beginning of a transformation in themselves, their colleagues, and even their students' beliefs and thoughts. That transforms their communication with each other and their daily behaviors and actions toward their goals.

The way the self-talk agents work is simple. When you hear Perfection Patty start to whisper, "This isn't good enough. It has to be perfectly planned," you simply call on her rival, Try-It-Out Trevor, and say, "You know what Patty? I am brave enough to try new things, and it might work. But it also might not work, and I will learn lessons through trial and error."

Or when Overwhelm Olivia raises her voice and shouts, "I can't believe how much there is to do today! I don't know where to start, so what's the point?" You can calmly ask Step-by-Step Sabrina to take the floor and say back, "Yes, there's a lot to do, but I will focus on what will create the biggest impact on my vision for myself and my people."

And that's how the self-talk agents work. When you hear them step in, ask yourself, "Is this an Agent of Same talking, or an Agent of Change?" You can then identify your next best step.

As you build your self-awareness and teacher brand based on how you believe, think, talk, and act, you will become more aware of how you can be proactive about your day's challenging parts. Use your awakened sense of awareness, and you can prepare yourself for the hard stuff before it happens. When a personal or professional challenge arises, take a deep breath and ask yourself questions about your brand. Here are examples:

What are my core values as I walk into this meeting that I don't want to go to? How do I want to leave my mark, if any, on this meeting? How am I projecting my core values?

Before I engage with this incredibly tough class, how would someone with my mission statement react when James becomes disruptive, or Sheila doesn't have her work done?

What can I say, if anything, that is helpful and not harmful?

Images 2.2 and 2.3: You may find it helpful to use the Agents of Change with students to help them change their self-talk. This is an essential step in building a growth mindset. Photo credit: Nicole Eveland.

In the next Hack, we'll go even deeper into reflecting on your challenges, but this is a great place to start shedding light on your most challenging people or moments of the day. As you figure that out, you can pre-build your responses based on the teacher brand you're building.

STEP 3: Understand your habits (who, what, where, when, and why).

Habits are essential now, and as you continue to move out of burnout. We aren't talking about the habits you complete on total recall, like brushing your teeth or answering the phone with "Hello?" To change your current reality, you've got to change your impact habits. Just like you have to control your brain and change the way you talk to yourself, you must change the habitual way you engage with and impact others, where you spend most of your time, and when and why you do the things you do.

Who? Who do you hang out with the most? Why? Do they affect your teacher brand positively or negatively?

What? What do you regularly think, do, and say that affect your burnout?

Where? Where do you spend most of your time? Do you have a habit of hanging out in the hallway for too long, hindering your ability to get things done? How does where you hang out affect your brand?

When? When do you make time to work on your teacher brand and personal development? Do you have a habit of saying, "I'll do it tomorrow"?

Why? Why do you have the habits that you do, and how could they be attributed to your burnout?

STEP 4: Avoid "The Crab Mentality."

Now that you're aware of your burnout type, stage, triggers, people, core values, and self-talk habits, I want to tell you about a theory called The Crab Mentality. I didn't make this up, and there are different variations of the same story, but my version goes like this:

One day, early in the morning, you decide to watch the sunrise on the beach. You arrive and begin to walk along the shore as the gentle waves lick your feet. As you walk, you notice a small crab crawling next to you. You quickly pick it up, as you know your kids would love to see a real, live crab. You get back to your rental, and you put it in a bucket while you wait for the children to wake up.

Hours pass, and as the kiddos wake, you excitedly rush them over to the bucket that you've placed on the back patio. However, when you peer over the side of the bucket, you find that the crab is gone.

You didn't know crabs could climb out of a bucket, but they can. At some point during the long wait, the crab clawed its way out and safely returned to the sea. You promise them that tomorrow, you will wake them up early and take them to the beach (with a bucket) to catch crabs together as the sun rises.

And the next morning, crabs abound. The kids, although groggy at first, easily catch close to ten crabs and place them in the bucket together. Through the squeals of excitement, the children wait to see a crab climb the side of a bucket. But to your dismay, you and the children watch as again and again, each crab that tries to claw its way out is pulled down by the ones left in the bucket. This goes on for about fifteen minutes before your oldest child makes a plea for justice. "Let them out! They're going to hurt each other." So you do. And again, just like the crab from the day before, they return safely to the ocean.

You probably didn't know that if you had left the crabs in the bucket, and some continued to try to escape, the crabs eventually would have broken each other's arms and even committed crab homicide to keep each other in the bucket. This is what is known as The Crab Mentality. Alone, the crab was free to do what it knew was in its best interest. Climb out. Go home. Be safe.

However, when surrounded by other animals of the same species, that same crab would have been forced to remain in the bucket—forced to stay stuck among the chaos and torment, only to have its life threatened if it tried to do what it felt was best for him.

Now, we are not crabs. Nor are we confined in a bucket, striving to return to our ocean home. However, we can find ourselves surrounded by people who think, feel, and believe that their misery is, and should be, normalized by everyone around them. They also act as though anyone who has a different way of thinking, feeling, believing, or living should be pulled right back to where they belong—in their misery.

I call these people "tearer-downers."

A more difficult reality is when the people who love and care about us the most are scared because they see us acting outside of the usual go-with-the-flow mentality, and they tear us down to "keep us safe." With the best of intentions (to keep you safe from the harms that could befall you), they will list every reason under the sun for why you should stay where you are and continue business as usual.

Both scenarios are hard, hurtful, and downright scary. Luckily for you, you're not a crab, and you are gaining the skills necessary to step out of that "bucket" with pride, confidence, and a sense of validation and curiosity that you never knew you had.

STEP 5: Find your Top Five Influencers.

When you believe that you are worthy and capable of a different way of thinking, feeling, believing, and living, you will begin to feel like you need to surround yourself with new people. You need people who build you up rather than tear you down when you want to create new habits to better yourself.

It isn't easy to release past relationships. It can be extremely hard to cut ties with those who continuously raise your blood pressure with their victimized thoughts and words when you need someone to lower it. You will have to decide the best way to gently release these past friendships that, as it turns out, were built on your shared desire to bask in the warmth of misery together on your island of burnout. Since you're not a crab, living in the sand in a miserable climate isn't ideal for you or your future. At some point, you will choose to claw your way out silently, without drama or broken arms.

Choose to surround yourself with the people who build you up, support you, and inspire you. Select your Top Five Influencers from any combination of your current workplace, past workplaces, community, and your PLN.

Building or rebuilding a teacher brand isn't about becoming a different version of yourself, but rather a more self-aware and empowered version of yourself. Putting this Hack into action will require you to think, feel, believe, and do things that you either have never done or haven't done in a while. Addressing your brand is hard, and rebuilding is even harder. But with a strong foundation of understanding how you got to where you are (Hack 1) and now a better awareness of how you project yourself to your people (Hack 2), you can stand tall as you create changes in your world and move through the stages of burnout to become an empowered teacher.

OVERCOMING PUSHBACK

It's a lot to ask you to take a step back to look at yourself from a new angle. It takes courage to look at yourself in the mirror and ask the questions in this Hack. But creating better self-awareness is necessary if you want to identify and understand what habits you have built into your teacher brand. Those are the habits that are either attracting or repelling the builder-uppers that will keep pushing you forward on your journey out of burnout.

You must do something different to see different results. And some of these changes, especially in who you start or stop hanging around and things you start or stop saying, will produce raised eyebrows from your colleagues and students.

Teachers will think I'm stuck up if I don't hang out with them in the lounge or hallway anymore. I know this is a touchy subject. The teacher's lounge can be a popular place, where the popular teachers hang out to have their daily doom meetings. I rarely frequented the lounge in any of the schools I worked in because I quickly created a habit of conducting a working lunch and eating while I took care of business: grading, planning, or answering emails. I didn't see the point in sitting around and focusing on all the bad things that were happening, or what the principal had or hadn't been doing right. I had work to do, and those conversations weren't producing anything useful for my mindset.

If someone brings up the idea that you're not hanging out with them anymore, be polite and have a solid, honest reason for the changes you've made in where you spend your time. You can simply say that you've got to focus on your work so you can get home at a more decent time. You could also be bold and state that you are tired of having the same negative conversations and you're working on a teacher brand that focuses on what you can control and what truly matters: your students.

Trust me: the right teachers will get the message when you start attracting the more positive go-getter teachers who want to work hard for their students and families and have conversations that move everyone forward.

Trying to change is just a phase. People often make resolutions in January that quickly become fad-goals, swept under the rug as an afterthought by the beginning of February. But this isn't a resolution; this is your brand. You carry it with you everywhere you go. When your students or colleagues look at you with a "That's cute" when you tell them you're working on your brand, hold your head up high and call on an Agent of Change, Capable Carrie, and say, "I am capable and worthy of changing my brand, and this is going to have lasting effects on my career and life."

It's too hard to break my bad habits. I've had these thoughts and friends for over twenty years. Change is hard. Habits are hard to break. But it can be done with five little words: "I don't do that anymore." You created your habits from your beliefs, and beliefs are a choice. Choices can be changed, but it takes being intentional every day about where you go, who you hang out with, and what you say and do. Of course, you still can have a good old vent session with your best friend when one of your students pukes on your phone (yes, that happened to me). But this is about self-awareness and your consistent beliefs, thoughts, words, and actions.

When you begin to say something unnecessarily negative about the teacher down the hall, tell yourself, "I don't do that anymore." When you get ready to share that negative meme about your principal with your group of teacher friends, tell yourself, "I don't do that anymore." When you begin to pile papers atop another pile of papers, tell yourself, "I don't do that anymore." You can even say this statement aloud to those who question why you politely excused yourself from a conversation that started going south about "that family." "I don't do that anymore."

It seems simple, but it is so effective.

THE HACK IN ACTION
By Chris Y., strategic learning coordinator

I was the kid who never knew what he wanted to be when he grew up. Then I started coaching high school wrestling in college and enjoyed that job. Late in my college career, I switched majors to biology education. I ended up getting my first teaching job and felt guilt almost immediately. I enjoyed my job, but compared to many teachers, I did not live to teach. Unlike others, I did not plan to be a teacher from the time I entered kindergarten. Despite enjoying what I was doing and having a good connection with students, I felt inadequate because I did not share the same level of passion that I saw in many colleagues.

I was destined to be a part of that statistic where teachers leave the classroom ... until I saw how teaching with technology impacted my students and my classroom. It quickly became my passion. Students were telling other teachers about the fun we were having, and I presented at staff meetings. I was making a difference in my school building and impacting more students than ever. At the same time, I was also being passed up for roles to follow this newfound passion full time. I was passed up by my district and others. I was passed up because I didn't have a brand beyond my building.

Whether we want to admit it or not, every teacher has a reputation or a brand—a reputation amongst students, staff, and community. The thing about a reputation is that if we're unwilling to share purposefully, then we have little control over what that reputation looks like.

It's challenging to be rejected while following your passion, but it is also incredibly motivating. I valued sharing how I loved to teach, with the hopes that students would love to learn. To avoid being passed up again, I knew I needed to build a brand that represented the fun and learning that students and I were having and doing in the classroom, and beyond that, I needed to be vulnerable enough to share it with the world.

I found like-minded edu folks to bounce ideas off of, and we started a PLN we branded as EdTech Heroes. I started sharing the daily happenings of my classroom on Twitter. I presented at local and state conferences. I never passed up an opportunity to spread my message.

At the same time, I knew I needed to stand out, but do it while also being true to myself. I had always been passionate about sneakers, and it was a common bond that I shared with my students. In my classroom "safe space," I wore the craziest sneakers. Anytime I went beyond my classroom, though, I would morph into this "Professional Chris" version of myself that I thought others expected me to be as a teacher. It took me a while to realize that you must be authentically you when you are building your brand.

Once I accepted who I was, what I valued, and where I wanted to be, everything changed. I found success, and my values spread beyond my school building. I was offered my dream job in my current district. One of the districts that passed up on me asked me to keynote their conference shortly after that original interview. Everything happened so quickly because I was just being me. Even though it's sometimes incredibly hard to do, there's nobody better at being you than you. Embrace the uniqueness of you, and then be vulnerable enough to go out and share it.

Sometimes, the only thing harder than being in burnout and losing who you are is not feeling that you can be your true self. It's especially difficult when you realize you're not where you want to be in your career and life because you've convinced yourself that no one will accept you the way you are. When you do things differently and begin to let your brand shine through, you will turn heads.

Others may question you, but these are chances for you to become more self-aware and reflect on your core values, your people, and your brand. When life gets hard, it gives you opportunities to learn lessons and grow.

HACK 3

R: REFLECT AND TAKE ACTION ON YOUR CHALLENGES
RISE FROM CHALLENGES AND SEEK SOLUTIONS

Highly proactive people don't blame circumstances, conditions, or conditioning for their behavior. Their behavior is a product of their own, conscious choice.
— STEPHEN COVEY, AUTHOR

THE PROBLEM: YOU FEEL YOU'RE ALWAYS PUTTING OUT FIRES

IN A TEACHER's life, the challenges are vast. They are seemingly unending, and they come from different directions and show up unexpectedly every hour, day, and week.

When I was teaching, I remember hearing and saying, "I feel like all I did today was put out fires." Many teachers regularly say those words. When I was in college, I don't remember taking a firefighting course, do you?

What makes this high-alert, high-stress statement so valuable to pay attention to is that when you feel like you're always "on"—putting out those fires—you also feel like you don't have time to figure out where the fire started in the first place. In the constant rush, your once-voluntary fire for teaching can be smothered into a pile of smoldering ashes and smoke (Stage 0 of burnout).

Some students come into our classrooms hungry, tired, and grumpy, therefore creating a ripple effect of starter fires throughout the morning: treating other students poorly, not staying on task, falling asleep, treating us poorly. Student behavior is burning you out.

Some parents respond in unfavorable ways when we contact them, therefore creating a burning sensation in our very souls because they "should" do more to support their child who is struggling. Parent behavior is burning you out.

Some administrators are seemingly disconnected from what we deal with each day and promptly return students to class when we've removed them for disruptive behavior. Paperwork is flowing, and we can't keep up with the demands of making sure every t is crossed and every i is dotted on every page we must fill out, sign, and return at the proper time and with the proper care. Administration and paperwork are burning you out.

Take a deep breath and know this: burnout is an effect, not a cause.

Now obviously, cause and effect is a pattern that elementary teachers are familiar with, as we teach plot and problem/solution: every effect produces a cause, affecting other beings in the story, which causes other things to happen until the main cause is solved at the end.

Maybe I already listed the causes of your frustration and burnout, and maybe you have others. Either way, give these causes the attention they deserve, focus on what you can and can't control, and work toward seeking and finding solutions.

Are you burned-out for one of the following reasons?

- You desire to leave the grade level you're teaching.

- Your relationship with administration isn't how you wish it to be.

- You work so hard and so much that you don't know what to do with yourself when you have free time.

- You work long hours.

- Your students have no ambition.

- You have an increasing number and intensity of behavior issues that you don't feel trained for or prepared to handle.

> **LET GO OF THOUGHTS AND ACTIONS THAT FOCUS ON THE CHALLENGES RATHER THAN ON SOLUTIONS.**

What typically happens when we try to address these things that are making our lives as teachers hard is that we get to the statement about them and stop there. We do nothing differently. It may seem hard to know where to start to solve them, but the solution is to think, plan, and then take action. This Hack will help you do the thinking and planning, but you must take action to start seeing results.

THE HACK: REFLECT AND TAKE ACTION ON YOUR CHALLENGES

Reflecting and taking action on your challenges means identifying challenges as soon as they arise. It's about choosing what to focus on and what to do about the challenges. Do that, and you can begin to solve the problem by actively engaging in each challenge.

First, get still and quiet. Rid yourself of the distractions around you so you can think back. Way back. Recall, in Hack 1, when we reflected on how long you've been in "this place" (physically, mentally, or emotionally). Now we're taking the work you did in your physical, mental, and emotional stance a step further.

You have to dive deeper than, "My administrator has been making my teaching life so hard since he started here two years ago" or "My students are so disrespectful. They've changed over the last twenty years" or "I've been working sixty-five-plus hours a week for three years, and I can't do this anymore."

Next, you'll have to let go of thoughts and actions that focus on the challenges rather than on solutions. Because sometimes what you continue to hold onto is what is holding you back. They're keeping you in burnout, and if you want to begin to move *out* of burnout, you must get out of your comfort zone.

Get past the "I can't change this" barrier. You may be saying, "I'm *far* from comfortable. I hate where I work and can't relate to these kids. They make me uncomfortable every day." You might be saying, "Really, Amber. You wouldn't believe the amount of paperwork that comes my way each day. I look at that stack at the beginning of each day, and it grows with every minute. You can't possibly understand what I'm dealing with here."

You're right. I don't know what you're dealing with specifically at your school or in your classroom. No one knows your challenges better than you. Therefore, *you* get to be the solution. *You* get to find a way. *You* get to reflect on your challenges and decide on your solutions.

In this Hack, you will learn the value of internalizing previous Hacks and acting on them before moving to the next step. I'm going to push you to take actions that will move you further out of your comfort zone and closer to becoming an empowered teacher.

WHAT **YOU** CAN DO TOMORROW

I've heard it said that a goal without action is just wishful thinking. The same holds true for addressing challenges and seeking solutions. Stating the challenges you're facing is the beginning of what has to happen for you to be a true solution-seeker.

- **Create a list.** Are you ready to start seeing solutions as you write things down? Great! We're going to make two lists: one each for personal and professional challenges. Let it all out. Take those thoughts, frustrations, worries, and things that cause you daily stress and put them somewhere other than your brain. Write down all of the challenges that clutter and fog your mind. You can even go back to childhood if you see the need. Are you already solving your problems?

- **Ask "why?"** Narrow down the root cause of the problems that you're having, both professionally and personally, by asking yourself why this thing is a challenge to you. Ask why over and over again to get to the root of that challenge. Here's an example:

"The long hours are burning me out."

Why?

"Because I'm always exhausted and can't do anything that I love doing."

Why?

"Because I'm a high school English teacher and I always have around 120 essays to grade at the end of each grading period, plus I'm the department chair, coaching two sports, and am also PTO president."

Why?

"Because I was promoted to department chair, I've always coached, and when I was asked to be PTO president, I felt bad saying no—even though I didn't want to do it."

Do you see where this is going? You also could ask someone you trust or your burnout buddy to push you to answer the question "Why?" Doing so will offer you a new perspective and give you possible solutions moving forward.

- **Ask, "Can I or can't I control this?"** Part of seeking solutions is deciding which challenges you should spend your precious time trying to solve. As much as you'd like to, you cannot solve some challenges. So you must decide which ones you can let go. Overthinking and replaying stressful situations (both past and present) that are out of your control will cause you to call on the same negative thoughts you've been thinking to yourself. It will also cause your brain to look for more problems associated with those situations.

Things outside of your control:

- Anything from the past
- Your students' upbringing
- Your students' choices
- Your administration and colleagues' beliefs and choices
- Natural disasters
- Your memories

Things within your control:

- Who you allow to influence you (your Top Five Influencers from the last Hack)
- Your focus on solutions
- Your preparation
- Your reactions to your administration's, colleagues', and students' choices
- Your effort
- Your attitude

- **Find trends in your challenges.** Is it possible that by finding ways to resolve or minimize one challenge, you're able to check off a few others that are related to or directly caused by that challenge?

- **Seek solutions and fellow solution-seekers.** For those challenges that you can control, write down all the possible solutions. And don't hold back. Dream big. Every challenge has many possible solutions in any situation.

  Unfortunately, if one or more of your challenges results from someone else's actions, thoughts, or beliefs, you must decide if you're going to rise above it, change your perspective, or get away from it. When dealing with these challenges, it is your choice regarding what you let roll off your back and what you separate from yourself. Consider these ideas before making this decision.

  Seek out people who could potentially help you and offer possible solutions to your challenges. These people can provide a different perspective to help you move away from previous biases and beliefs about how things "should" be.

  Identify challenges that you are *not* in control of, and either jot down how you plan to rise above them, change your perspective about them, or get away from them altogether. Stressing about things you truly can't control is not healthy. Losing sleep over uncontrollable challenges won't solve them, and it certainly won't help you to be your best self in the morning.

- **Assume positive intent with everyone, yet have the hard conversations when necessary.** Positive intent means believing that when people say or do things, they mean well and are doing the best they can at the moment. We'd like to think we know every fact about everyone in our lives, but we don't. We don't know what happened last night, this morning, or five minutes ago in people's lives. News of a sick friend or family member, an argument, a stubbed toe, sleep deprivation, or any such circumstance will sometimes surface as a snippy or snide remark, side-eye, or an unwarranted tantrum—with us on the other end. And this also includes our students. We sometimes hold a bias about our students' day-to-day lives. We sometimes take our beliefs about their lives and compare them to our childhood or our biological children's lives.

   We're all fighting our own battles with different people and situations. Some people are not the type who would seek a shoulder to cry on or a hug. Some people process loss, grief, overwhelm, and exhaustion differently, and it's up to us to show grace and positive intent when people don't treat us the way we treat them, or when they don't go about something the way we would.

   However, when you hear snide remarks or what you perceive as rude comments and acts of malice against you, it is up to you to stick up for yourself and call a meeting. These hard conversations don't have to be defensive or negative. They simply can be started with, "Can you help me understand what you meant when you said (or did)...?"

When you come from a place of seeking to understand, it sets you and the other person up for success. And this goes for conversations with your students, too. We make assumptions that people's actions toward us have everything to do with us, when, many times, angry words and actions have less to do with us and everything to do with what happened before the words or actions emerged.

Avoiding these hard conversations means ignoring an opportunity to improve relationships, which, in turn, can directly affect your growth out of burnout.

**Note: If you're dealing with discrimination, abuse, or bullying of any kind in any of your challenges, this is a call to action. If you're wondering if your burnout is a more severe illness, please tell someone who can help you take care of you and your situation. I'm no psychologist or doctor. I'm an educator serving educators. If your health or safety is in jeopardy, seek professional help. Put down this book and make the call.

A BLUEPRINT FOR FULL IMPLEMENTATION

This Hack helps you begin to act differently in the face of adversity: to seek solutions rather than focusing solely on the challenge, and to look inside yourself and figure out what you're willing to do to make things better.

STEP 1: Practice serenity and radical acceptance.

The serenity prayer isn't just for addicts. Although popularized by Alcoholics Anonymous in the early 1940s, the serenity prayer's author and origin are contested.

> "God, give me the serenity to accept the things I cannot change, the courage to change the things I can, and the wisdom to know the difference."

In a profession full of self-diagnosed people-pleasers and control freaks, the serenity prayer, put into consistent practice, can help us remember that we are only in control of our own lives, and we can't make choices for other people. We have to accept their choices as reality. One way to fight the burnout of continually putting out fires, as I mentioned earlier, is to identify what you can and cannot change, and what does and does not need controlling.

You can't change that Kaitlin came into your classroom, pushed Austin to the ground, and then slammed her backpack into her cubby, but you can control how you react to the situation. It's your choice whether you yell at her from across the room or walk up to her calmly to find out why she is upset. It takes courage to stay calm and seek understanding, but sometimes small flames are quickly fanned into larger ones by our reactions as teachers.

Calling on Human Hannah from Hack 2 will help you remember that you're not a superhero, cannot save everyone, and do not have to act alone.

The practice of accepting things that you cannot change is called "radical acceptance" and will be extremely helpful as you internalize and practice serenity. Radical acceptance, as defined by psychologist Marsha Linehan, is "about accepting life on life's terms and not resisting what you cannot or choose not to change. Radical acceptance is about saying yes to life, just as it is."

That's it. Acknowledging that you disagree with the way things are, whether it's how a child is being raised or the injustice and inequality you witness within our education system. Perhaps these challenges ignite such passion inside you that you decide you *will* try to change them. But if you choose not to change systems or policies, that is also a choice, and you must accept it and move on to focus on what you can control: your attitude, habits, and effort.

That's not to say you will sit idly by while you witness your students bully one another or don't speak up when you hear another teacher make a racist remark about a new family that just started at your school. Social injustice is everywhere, and when you have the opportunity to stand up for your fellow humans, whether they're students, teachers, or administrators, take it. Use common sense when deciding whether you could or should do something about a challenging situation, which takes us to the next step.

STEP 2: Stop the subjunctives (shoulda, coulda, woulda).

I'm not going to sugarcoat this. Life's hard. It even sucks sometimes. We make mistakes that have negative impacts on our lives and perhaps on the lives of other people. However, we have to stop listening to the voices in our heads (or from our mouths) that consistently blame our poor choices or others' bad decisions on our current reality. That's called "living in the subjunctive."

The subjunctive is defined as "Designating or of the mood of a verb that is used to express supposition, desire, hypothesis, possibility, etc., rather than to state an actual fact" (Webster's New World College Dictionary).

The English language is one of only a few that even have subjunctives. Therefore, if you were to travel to some countries and talk about how, "If the guy sitting next to me wouldn't have sneezed on my sleeve, I wouldn't have a runny nose," they'd have no idea what you meant by your negative if/then statement. The fact is, it *did* happen, and now you must carry tissues.

There isn't enough money in the world to change what has happened in the past. The only thing we can control is how we accept, forgive, and appreciate our decisions, or those of others, as lessons learned. We can feel grateful that we have the human capacity to move on and make better choices in the future.

So, before you open your mouth to say statements like these, stop yourself:

- "If people making the policies and standards would spend a day in education, they would know how hard this job is and how unrealistic their expectations are."

- "I wish I could just take these kids home with me and show them how a 'normal' family behaves."

- "If only my principal would spend a day in my class, she would know how ridiculous her new school-wide initiative is."

- "If only I had a degree in interior design, then I would be happier and richer."

Decide if you can control the situation, why it's challenging you, and if you can spend your time and energy on more proactive solutions such as understanding state policies and standards and how they came to be, or working on eliminating or shrinking your biases about what is "normal."

STEP 3: Check your personal and professional bias.

We bring our own steadfast beliefs about what is right versus wrong, normal versus abnormal, good versus bad, and acceptable versus unacceptable into a classroom full of younger human beings who have their own worldviews of what is right, normal, good, and acceptable. We must continually call on and react to our unconscious biases about our students' behavior and how their parents or others are raising them.

We may have beliefs toward our administrators, who have their own biases of what a good versus bad classroom management structure looks like or appropriately or inappropriately written lesson plans.

When we don't take time to acknowledge our own bias and how it affects our view of our people and the people we work for and with, we lose opportunities to learn about why our students, their families, and our coworkers do and say the things they do.

Our beliefs are the reason we can't imagine a student calling us a "stupid b-word." It's why we crumble when we're told to deal with it, as we fight the tears that want to flow because our feelings were hurt.

Little did we know that this language is acceptable in some homes and is even encouraged by families who don't see a problem with using explicit language regularly—cue radical acceptance. Whether it goes beyond your beliefs of "appropriate," I encourage you to think more deeply about the language and what caused the student to use it.

Coming from a place of understanding before trying to be understood is one of the easiest ways to keep yourself from allowing your bias to overtake your emotions and turn a molehill into a mountain.

When your jaw drops because you see or hear something that *never* would have been allowed in your home, or when your principal is making a bias assumption about your teaching methods, let go of the subjunctive and practice radical acceptance. Seek to understand by using this sentence stem:

"Can you help me understand ...?"

Any time you find yourself facing a challenge, first seek to understand. It will change everything.

In the book *Hacking School Discipline*, authors Nathan Maynard and Brad Weinstein describe how to better understand student behavior by asking questions. "We need to figure out how to hear student voices, rather than just using one-size-fits-all treatments for discipline. To do this, we need to seek to understand behaviors instead of just labeling them and assigning consequences. That means that immediately after a negative behavior occurs, we start with a series of open-ended questions:

- What happened?

- What were you thinking about when _____ happened?

- Who did this affect, and how so?"

Asking these questions can alleviate the pain of being called a nasty name. You're focusing on understanding the students' immediate challenge rather than taking it personally and thinking you know their challenge in the first place.

STEP 4: Focus on the solutions, not the problem.

What you believe is your reality. When you think you don't have enough time or money, then you will not have enough. When you believe that your problems are so vast you can't even begin to try to solve them, it will be your reality.

Whether you call it manifesting, autosuggestion, or the scientific term Reticular Activating System, it all means the same thing. Whatever you choose to focus on will show up in your life. The more you think, feel, or believe something to be true, the more it will show up.

A scarcity mindset—the belief that there isn't and won't be enough—causes us to hoard empty butter dishes and cereal boxes and dead markers. We've convinced ourselves that we will need them someday—and in fact, we'll find a way to use them, even if it isn't practical.

But if you choose to believe that there is more than enough time and money because you've adopted an abundance mindset, the belief that there is plenty for everyone and more will be coming will also be true.

Choosing an abundance mindset does not excuse being wasteful with resources, time, or energy, but instead allows you to be grateful for them. Nor does sharing ideas, materials, smiles, and gratitude mean that you should give away all of yourself until nothing is left.

The second my husband and I decided we wanted to buy a

Subaru Outback and left the dealership to go home and research them ... guess what? We started seeing Subaru Outbacks everywhere. Our brains were on high alert for that thing we wanted, and that's what we saw. Whether or not you *want* hardship, if you choose to focus on the problem rather than on the solutions, you will continue to find hardship.

When you list your challenges, that is an exercise to help you also list your solutions. Move on from there and become a seeker of those solutions, because when you set out to seek solutions, eventually solutions are what you will find.

STEP 5: Become a seeker of solutions.

We're teachers, and we solve problems all day—especially problems for other people.

- "Who's going to sit where?"

- "Okay, Abby's partner isn't here today, so who will she work with?"

- "My kid is sick, my partner is on a business trip, and I have a field trip today. What to do?"

Those surface-level, in-the-moment problems take a lot out of us when they are stacked on top of each other all day, every day. No wonder we don't want to deal with these deeper, more impactful issues that are slowly causing us to question our existence as educators.

Well, that all changes now. You are going to transform yourself from a problem-finder to a solution-seeker—no slapping a Band-Aid on a gaping wound here. We're taking time to clear out the infection, stitch that puppy back up, and keep that wound from reopening.

Refer to the list of challenges you made earlier and recall which ones could have residual problem-solving effects on other challenges you're having.

STEP 6: Physically sit inside your challenges and possible solutions.

Now it's time to physically sit inside these challenges and solutions, and see how you feel as you're doing it.

1. Highlight/identify your Top Five challenges and write each one on a separate piece of paper or index card.

2. Sit on the floor and surround yourself with a circle of these challenges.

   • How do you feel?

   • What do you notice?

   • Take a selfie from above to give you perspective. Write down how your body is reacting.

3. Go through the same practice with your solutions. Write your Top Five on separate pieces of paper and set them all around you.

   • Read them out loud.

   • Take a picture from above.

   • How do you feel now that you have considered solutions to these challenges? You may have noticed that by surrounding yourself with both

your challenges and solutions, you put yourself
in control of which one (the challenge or the
solution) you will allow to affect you the most.
Hopefully, you choose to be affected by the solutions, because having a positive outlook moving
forward will transform your mindset and allow
you to make giant gains out of burnout.

Of course, seeking solutions is only a step in the right direction.
You have to act. And that can be the hardest part. In Hack 6, we'll
go through a deeper practice to prioritize and set action steps to
solve these problems for good.

OVERCOMING PUSHBACK

As you train your brain to focus on solutions at the root of why
issues are challenging you, you will find it easier to decide whether
a challenge is worth your time and energy to solve, or if you should
take a deep breath, release the shoulda, coulda, woulda, and move
on. But you'll experience pushback, so it's best to be prepared.

I have no support. Perhaps this was true before you picked up
this book. But now you know that support is out there. You may
just need to look for it somewhere other than the places you've been
inhabiting. Your range of support can be as far-reaching as you want
it to be, but you must align your needs with what you're seeking.
Thousands of Facebook groups are out there, for example, but if
they aren't offering you what you truly need, leave them. They'll still
be around later if that's the type of support you need in the future.
Find a place that *does* offer you the right kind of support.

**It's selfish of me to ignore the injustices I see happening
in education.** Radical acceptance isn't about agreeing with the

injustice and lack of equity that we see occurring consistently in education; it's about choosing what you want to invest in changing and what you don't. So if you can't stop thinking about the inequitable funding of school districts, and the thought of going into politics intrigues you, and you can see yourself advocating for more equitable practices by our government—go for it! If you're passionate about this, why not you?

However, if you don't desire to take steps to create actual change in school funding, then you're choosing not to. That's not selfish; it's just how you choose to spend your time. You choose to impact the students in your classroom and teach them to advocate for equity now and in the future.

Focusing on solutions is a waste of time. Someone or something will come along and ruin my plans. Maybe, but maybe not. Focusing on solutions to your biggest challenges, after determining why they are challenging you, will boil down to the changes you need to make in yourself, your expectations, bias, and current practices. If you're focusing on changes and solutions within your circle of control, no one should be able to touch them.

I'm powerless, and there's not enough time. I can't change anything. Remember, what you believe becomes your truth. If you choose to believe you're powerless to change anything about the challenges you regularly deal with, your brain will find ways to prove that it's true. It will also find ways to prove there isn't enough time to find solutions to your problems.

But isn't that how we got here in the first place? By letting challenges build up without slowing down to attend to them? It's your choice to believe in a scarcity of time or that you're powerless; however, you can make a new choice.

You can choose to believe that you're powerful, capable, and worthy of changing parts of your reality. If your main challenge is your self-talk, then I suggest that you spend time each day saying positive things about yourself and your power. Print out the Agents of Change posters or listen to positive affirmations on YouTube.

THE HACK IN ACTION
By Rachael G., classroom teacher

I went into my third year of teaching, expecting to be the queen of the world. I had heard it was to be a magical year full of smooth sailing and engaging lesson plans. As I was preparing for the year, though, I realized there had been a clerical mistake when a student was enrolled the previous year. I taught in a high-migrant/ESL population school, and due to the language barrier, a student had been put into the incorrect grade. By the time they got to me, I realized I had a seven-year-old with limited English and no educational foundation in my third grade class.

I immediately went to my principal. Something had to change…but nothing did. So I went above my principal. I went to everyone. If you had ears, you heard about the injustices in my classroom: the student shouldn't be in my room, my other students were being disserviced, my administration didn't like me anymore—the list went on.

Things reached an apex around parent-teacher conferences. I tried my best to show how I was working to help the students in my room, but the parents saw it differently. They asked questions about why their child was in certain differentiated groups when their scores didn't reflect those needs. At that point, I could no longer approach my administration without needing to convene a council. Whenever I needed to meet about a student, the meeting included my principal, my assistant principal, my union rep, and another building rep. I felt like the Titanic. No sharp turns or you might hit an iceberg. It was terrible. I felt miserable. My students weren't getting the education they needed from me. I was doing them a disservice.

At this point in my life, my teaching career needed a hard reset.

I left the classroom midyear and took a position in a different district. I worked to help restart and reset their English as a New Language program. It was also an opportunity for me to reset my teaching career.

I realized that I needed to be a better listener. So many aspects of my new position were less than ideal. Teachers were not fans of the changes, but I had to make this new position work. I realized there are times when it is better to nod my head and smile and continue doing what I'm doing. Radical acceptance, here I go. I chose to be a better listener; to learn to empathize; to realize that everyone, even administration, has a perspective and faces challenges in their position. No single person in education can make all the challenges go away.

Once I accepted that and learned to become a better listener and empathizer, I was able to shift my mindset and understand what I needed to do to feel more fulfilled in my position, rather than burning out.

Reflecting on past challenges is okay, but when we look at our past mistakes or misunderstandings as opportunities to know and do better, we gain valuable learnings. You can fail, but you can't be a failure, because failure is an experience (and a highly valuable one), not a way of being. You've likely heard the saying, "You either win, or you learn."

Learning lessons is part of life, and being wise doesn't come from being perfect. It comes from being able to say confidently, "I messed up, and I'm taking with me the lesson learned from that mistake." Instead of burning out, reflect on and address your challenges ... and then learn from them and continue your journey forward.

HACK 4

N: NURTURE YOUR HABITS AND STRENGTHS

LEARN WHAT MAKES YOU GREAT AND HOW YOUR HABITS BRING OUT OR HINDER YOUR GREATNESS

Habit is ten times nature.

— Duke of Wellington Arthur Welles

THE PROBLEM: YOU DON'T REALIZE THE IMPACT OF YOUR HABITS ON YOUR NATURAL STRENGTHS

How many times have you heard yourself or a colleague say one of the following statements?

"I'm a Type A and a total control freak. I just want to control everything."

"I'm a perfectionist and always have been."

"I want everyone to like me, and I'm a total people-pleaser."

"I know it's not a good habit, but I can't help but ..."

Being a perfectionist, people-pleasing, or a control freak has become the routine in some schools, and it's almost a rite of passage to being a teacher. Thanks to social media and search engines, you can find many ways to color code, label, and use a custom font for every file, drawer, and worksheet you'll ever encounter. Saying yes immediately, before thinking about whether you have the time, skills, and desire to do what someone asked you to do, is often assumed and expected.

Slowly but surely, you've been falling into those traps and building harmful habits based on what you think pleases other people and looks good on Instagram, rather than developing healthy habits that soothe your teacher soul and allow you to tap into your natural strengths and abilities.

Also, you may have adopted unhealthy habits based on your beliefs about your time and worthiness. They are impeding your ability to achieve the growth necessary to get out of burnout. Have you found yourself adopting the following habits as "just the way teaching is"?

- Planning, prepping, and grading on nights and weekends

- Staying up too late and getting up at the very last minute

- Putting everything and everyone ahead of your well-being

- Teaching, planning, and grading the way you always have, because, well, you just always have

- Spending time beating yourself up about your weaknesses instead of knowing or focusing on your strengths

- Adopting the practices of other teachers (even though they're inefficient and ineffective) because you don't want to offend them

- Staying late because everyone else does, and you don't want them to judge you

These beliefs and habits are keeping you stuck in a perpetual state of anxiety and burning you out. Of course, you won't have time to do things differently if you've convinced yourself that these beliefs and habits are just the way things are and that you're powerless to change them.

Your Strengths and Personality Type

If I ask you to tell me your personality type, what comes to your mind first? Type A? Type B? What are your top strengths? What comes naturally to you and doesn't take much effort?

If you label yourself as a control freak without diving deeper into your personality and top strengths, you'll stick with the unhealthy habits that perpetuate your Type A status. You'll just keep on with that burnout.

Knowing the relationship between habits and strengths is essential to *beating* burnout. If you know your strengths yet don't have healthy habits to help you nurture them, you may waste them. If you have healthy habits, on the other hand, but don't recognize your strengths or look for opportunities to use them, you run the risk of becoming frustrated and bored—leading to burnout.

As teachers, we must take time to address how our beliefs have grown into bad habits that act as a weed killer to our strengths, which beg for us to water and nurture them so they can grow. We need to address both our strengths and habits to get ourselves out of burnout and into a healthy life.

THE HACK: NURTURE YOUR HABITS AND STRENGTHS

Knowing our strengths and weaknesses is only the start. We also must pay attention and analyze our everyday habits—and I'm not talking about brushing your teeth or biting your nails. I'm talking about habits that influence our ability (or inability) to take the time to focus on our strengths and weaknesses, reflect on our challenges, understand our teacher brand, and acknowledge how we got burned-out in the first place. To beat burnout, we must heighten our awareness of our current habits. See the self-awareness phase in Hack 2.

As a teacher working to beat burnout, you must take your self-awareness to a new level by identifying your habits, strengths, and weaknesses so you're better-equipped to make decisions about your next action steps on your journey out of burnout. You can do this by investing time (and maybe a bit of money) to analyze your daily habits and routines and take strengths and personality assessments. These will give you a good idea of where you are … and how to build those strengths with healthier habits.

Don't sell yourself short. It doesn't matter what stage of life or burnout you're in, how long you've been teaching, or how many students you have in your classroom or your family—you can learn new habits and grow your strengths. You need to do both to get out of burnout and become BURNED-IN.

WHAT YOU CAN DO TOMORROW

- **List your habits.**

  1. Make a T Chart. Write "professional" on one side and "personal" on the other.

  2. Write down habits that you find yourself completing daily in your personal and professional life.

     Personal life example:
     - Waking up at 5 a.m. for a workout
     - Skipping breakfast
     - Drinking three sodas a day
     - Cooking dinner three times a week for the family
     - Going to bed at midnight

     Professional life example:
     - Committing to one extracurricular activity each year (robotics coach, team lead, cross country coach)
     - Giving everyone you walk by in the hallway a high-five during the day
     - Spending your lunch hour venting in the teachers' lounge about "that one kid"

- Scrolling Instagram or Facebook during prep period
- Checking off your weekly list of to-dos each Thursday afternoon and knowing what you need to do before you leave on Friday

Refer back to Hack 2, where you reflected on your habits regarding who, what, where, when, and why. These are habits. Every one of them. What habits are holding you back? Which ones make you feel strong, empowered, and proud?

- **Take a personality assessment or two.** Whether you choose to take one or many personality assessments, take time to analyze your results and look for patterns in your behavior. Record your analysis and consider how you can use your findings to move forward on your journey out of burnout.

  Also, think about the challenges and their solutions that you listed in the last chapter. How can you utilize what you're learning about yourself to solve these challenges creatively?

A BLUEPRINT FOR FULL IMPLEMENTATION

An important step in changing your habits so you can nurture your strengths is to know what your strengths are and what habits can be changed. Habits are hard to break, and it takes intentional action to build new ones. The same is true of your strengths. If you want to spend more time doing the things that empower you, you must know what they are. Creating positive habits and nurturing strengths will get you out of burnout and turn you into a teaching powerhouse.

STEP 1: Do a daily habit analysis for one week.

What do you notice about how you spend your time, how you fuel your body and mind, and how often you're moving your body?

Analyze your morning habits.

- What time do you get up in the morning?
- What do you do directly after waking?
- When do you get to school, and how much time do you have before students arrive?

Analyze your afternoon habits.

- What time do you typically leave school?
- What do you do directly after school?
- When do you get home, and what do you do then?
- Do you have family members at home?
- What are your daily after-school habits and routines?

Analyze your evening habits.

- If you have young children, what time do you typically get your kiddos to bed at night?
- What are your habits before you go to sleep?
- What time do you usually fall asleep?

- How many hours of sleep do you get?

Analyze your weekend habits.

- What are your normal weekend activities?
- What do you do with friends and family?
- What weekend routines and habits make the next week run more smoothly?
- What do you do for fun?

Check-in.

- Are there items you have listed that take more time than they should?
- What do you do with your downtime? What are you eating and drinking regularly?
- How often are you intentionally moving your body?
- Is there a common theme to what you spend time on?
- Have you left time for personal growth and joy?
- Are you so worried about being productive that you're now working on autopilot and not feeling anything?
- Have you allowed yourself the brain space to look at your opportunities to grow?
- Do you have a choice in your involvement in any of these things?
- Are you happy?

As you analyze your habits for a week, you will see how your beliefs about time have created habits that make those beliefs true. Now that you have visible proof of your healthy or not-so-healthy habits, you can make room for learning more about yourself and your strengths.

STEP 2: Make sleep, eating healthy, and intentionally moving your body everyday priorities.

We all know it's essential to take care of ourselves. However, sometimes we confuse self-care with self-indulgence. While we may enjoy wine on Friday night and doughnuts on Saturday morning, it's important to balance them with a mostly healthy diet and active lifestyle.

Getting sleep, eating healthy, and moving your body are habits that don't have to be goal-driven. It doesn't have to be about losing twenty pounds or getting skinny. Eating right and exercising regularly also improve the mental health of anyone struggling with burnout, trauma, depression, and anxiety. And replacing lousy health habits with good ones will help you along your journey out of burnout. Now that you've evaluated your daily habits and routines, you can make adjustments in your health routines like:

1. Ditching old evening routines for ones that help everyone, especially you, get to bed earlier

2. Getting up a little earlier to run, walk, or practice yoga before school

3. Replacing your Diet Cokes with water—and lots of it

We all know old habits are hard to break, but if getting out of burnout is important to you, and I know it is, you will want to practice hourly and daily self-care by living a healthier lifestyle. A healthy life will strengthen your body and mind and help you nurture your strengths and find new ways to utilize them.

STEP 3: Take the Gallup CliftonStrengths assessment.

As teachers, we typically get evaluated three times a year. Yet, what do we tend to focus on? Our weaknesses. Of course, it's important to continue to reflect and grow our practice as educators, but if that's all we focus on, we're doing ourselves a disservice.

The Gallup CliftonStrengths assessment asks you questions that help you determine your unique talent DNA.

Read your results, print them, highlight phrases, circle words, and cross out irrelevant ideas. Ponder your results. Truly interact and come to understand them.

- What do you find as the most outstanding result?

- Did anything surprise you?

Your daily habits will determine your success (or failure) when it comes to achieving whatever you choose to do in life.

We all have skills to work on and skills to let shine. We all add value to the world, and that's why we explore your personality type and strengths to create habits that allow you the time to nurture your skills.

STEP 4: Build healthier habits around your commitments.

Now that you've analyzed the ins and outs of your daily routines and habits, you have found activities to start and stop doing. According to Amy Morin in *13 Things Mentally Strong People Don't Do*, "Putting other people first can also become a way to feel needed and important. So it becomes a habit to always invest energy into other people's feelings and lives."

You obviously can't tell your school administrators no when they add new students to your already-packed classroom, and you can't say no when a student with whom you've made tremendous progress moves away. But you can say no when asked to be part of something that doesn't align with your core values, mission statement, who you want to serve the most, and your goals.

You may have found yourself saying yes and no at the same time. You say yes to your peers and superiors for fear of letting them down, and you say no to your health, happiness, and family. Before you know it, you're over-extended and under-cared-for—again.

Suppose you've gotten into the habit of saying yes to every opportunity that comes your way, without stopping to think about whether it will build up your strengths or weaknesses, or whether you will enjoy it. In that case, this habit is holding you back from being able to say yes to opportunities that *can* help you grow and nurture your strengths.

Knowing how and when to say yes and no is not only a habit but a skill you can practice.

"No" is a powerful word. It's simple to say (to ourselves) and easy to spell, but why is it so difficult to get out of our mouths? We've made it culturally acceptable in our schools and classrooms to take on more responsibility with a smile and a nod. Others expect us to say yes when, inside, we're screaming, "Nooo!" But if you don't set healthy boundaries around your time, money, and energy, how can you expect other people to respect them?

If you are going to start saying yes to yourself, you need to be comfortable saying no to others. No doesn't have to be rude. It doesn't have to be loud. It just has to be verbalized. The following statements might come in handy:

- "I'm so flattered you thought of me, but I'm not going to be able to do this for you right now."

- "I've got other obligations right now. I won't be able to do that at this time." (And those obligations could be spending time at the park or pool, with or without the kids.)

- "You know, right now just isn't a good time. How about you ask me again in about six months? I may have more room in my schedule then."

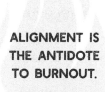

ALIGNMENT IS THE ANTIDOTE TO BURNOUT.

As you're deciding what you're going to say yes and no to, consider your current habits and your personal and professional goals and core values. For example, if your goal is to get out of burnout, and you realize one of the challenges you can control is how you feel physically, you can choose to say no to staying up too late and yes to getting up earlier for a workout. You can also say yes to drinking water all day instead of sugary soda and, instead, reward yourself with a treat once a week.

STEP 5: Practice positivity.

You can practice daily activities and habits to bring happiness into your life and routine. They take practice and intention but are helpful ways to turn a bad day around so you can focus on the good, even when life feels chaotic.

- Force a smile for fifteen seconds.

- Take three deep breaths before starting each class.

- Say, "I am happy, I am calm" or "I am confident, and I am taking action."

- Keep a note each day of funny or positive things to share with your partner, spouse, roommate, or mom on your way home from work or over dinner.

OVERCOMING PUSHBACK

But I'm good at leading that club or coaching that sport. If I stop, the new person won't be as good as I am. In *High Performance Habits*, Brendon Burchard writes, "What's achievable is not always what's important. You have a lot of things you CAN do. So the central question shifts from 'How do I achieve more?' to 'How would I like to live?' It's about realizing your thoughts and behaviors so that you can experience growth, well-being, and fulfillment as you strive."

When you think about how you want to live your life based on utilizing your strengths that light you up and the habits you need to improve to maximize them, you can let go of obligations that stretch you rather than grow you. Using your strengths for your people allows you to stick to your core values, and backed by your healthy habits and focus, this will create alignment. Alignment is the antidote to burnout.

As far as someone not being as "good" as you at something, I challenge you to think about why you believe that. Chances are, someone is better at coaching or leading that sport than you, which means that by letting someone else lead, you may be offering them a chance to use their strengths.

People will judge me for not being exhausted and leaving at my contract time. Eleanor Roosevelt said, "What other people think of me is none of my business," and I encourage you to adopt this mindset as you make your journey out of burnout. You're beginning to believe, think, feel, and behave differently than the status quo; therefore, others may judge and question you. However, as you bolster your strengths and habits, you will extend your reach and possibilities in new ways. You will open yourself up to new opportunities and new opinions from people who are not trying to drag you down and keep you the same.

When you start saying no to some or most of what you used to say yes to (working sixty-plus hours a week or being in charge or part of multiple committees and clubs), people will notice. You may even realize that some people are upset, and you will learn to be okay with this. Unfortunately, there are people who either intentionally or unintentionally take advantage of our inability to say no. The people who intentionally take advantage of you will question you when you set boundaries. Be prepared to advocate for yourself and let them know that you aren't mad, just overextended, and that you're working on setting boundaries so you can set aside time for rest and family (or your core values or reasons).

THE HACK IN ACTION
By Paula B., high school teacher

Change is the only constant in our lives, and learning to adapt or rebound from change can be mentally hard and can cause stress. As a teacher, I chose a career that continually moves, recycles, and changes. The changes happen by the year, the week, and mostly by the minute. All teachers can recite the staggering statistic that they make more than fifteen hundred decisions during a six-hour school day. No wonder we are so tired by the time the school bell rings. For me, that tiredness was more than being sleepy. My fatigue turned into long hours at school, negative self-talk, and worst of all, no energy left for my family or myself.

Even though my evaluations were positive, I felt like I was not doing the best job for my students. So, I spent hours rewriting the curriculum. Some days, I tweaked my lesson between classes so I could improve it before the next class. Perfection was my goal, and I was determined to achieve the perfect curriculum. Reflecting on my lessons became an obsession, and I needed to figure out an action plan to help my bad habit. I knew I had a problem because my job's stress and anxiety made it no longer fun. I love being a teacher, but at that time, I felt like I was drowning under the pressure of my self-doubt and the papers to grade, and with no time to care for my health or exercise. Friends and coworkers talked about my inner light and how bright I shine while walking the halls at school, but I knew my light would extinguish if I did not change. Burnout, for me, was inevitable if I did not act now.

I know one of my strengths is to build relationships with my students. Teaching is more than instructing students in the educational standards set forth by a state. Teaching requires the ability to nurture, counsel, identify, and, in my case, help solve the problems of teenage students. I am also a special education specialist because my district lacks intervention specialists, and sometimes I am a caregiver. Numerous times, I have supplied lunch money and gas money, and even picked up students from work in the evening because their parents would not.

I understood that it was unlikely to set boundaries with all students, but I could set boundaries and create systems for myself. I knew I needed to let go of situations out of my control and work together to solve problems we can control. I realized the seriousness of my situation when I started researching and looking for help. I looked for professionals to help me figure out how to manage my workload at school. I needed to change my mindset about my teaching career. I found professionals while watching a wellness summit and reading about growth mindset for my students. I listened to podcasts, read articles, and subscribed to professional publications. Teachers must model lifelong learning. I knew I needed help, and I always encouraged my students to ask for help, so I needed to follow my own advice. By researching and seeking out the help, I changed my habits.

My new habits and their outcome made a massive, unbelievable difference in my job. Teaching is my job, not my calling, but my objective was to give my students my best effort every day. Changing my mindset allowed me to create a curriculum, instruct my students, grade their work based on the objectives, and leave at the end of the day. By changing my mindset and following my plans, I am no longer reflecting on each lesson I teach. By looking at my assessments, I know where I need to reteach, and reteaching is fine with me now.

I also needed to make a conscious effort to stay away from the Negative Nellies in my building. Engaging in their negativity did not help my mindset. Now during my prep, before school and after school, I close my door and work. By doing this, I have added more positive productivity to my day and less negativity to my mind. I find great pleasure leaving the building and smiling while they are still standing in the hallway, chatting about what is wrong in their "school life."

My school is fortunate to have a wonderful and supportive IT department. One of my goals last year was to use our learning management system (LMS). Many of my students are in career technical programs, so they miss my class at times. I wanted to improve having my lesson plans and work for the week online and organized, so students would not miss anything in class if they were not there. I used the LMS to build weekly modules, so all my students could assess their work in one spot. Doing this alleviated the dreaded question, "What did we do in class yesterday?" All this self-reflection and overhauling of my classroom did not come without setbacks. Learning the LMS was not easy. On many days, I wanted to give up, but I remembered the stacks and stacks of papers that I used to have on my desks and the amount of wasted class time it would take to "catch up" a student the next day. Eventually, using the LMS became more manageable, and grading was the best. I no longer had to grade and then post grades to the grade book program. The LMS and our grade book program sync up. That, my friends, is the best feature for a person who assigns only short-answer questions and essays and hates to grade. Best teaching hack ever!

My best advice for coping with teacher burnout is facing it head-on. Identify your issues by asking yourself what you can control and what you cannot control. I identified that I managed the level of production in my lessons. My lessons were good enough, and if they were not, I could help those students separately. I did not need graphics and pictures and unique fonts to make my lessons visually pleasing. The content and how I delivered it were the critical parts. Having relationships with my students, showing them that learning is a lifelong process, and having fun in class were essential parts of my educational philosophy—that is why I teach.

Now, when thoughts of burnout creep into my mind, it is much easier to bounce back because I have a plan. I had a challenge, and I used research to overcome it. Plus, my professional learning community helped me see my strengths and create new habits to streamline many systems in my classroom. The outcome of my work is the method of looking into the mirror and asking myself the burning question: is this something I can control or not?

When you're burned-out, it's hard not to get sucked into negative beliefs and habits that drag you even deeper into burnout. So many options and temptations are out there to make you feel that you need to focus on the look of your lesson, rather than on whether the contents meet your students' needs, and whether it reflects your strengths and values as a teacher. Each fall, I see "classroom reveals" on social media, and I cringe. Their rooms are adorable, and all the fonts match on their worksheets—yet I hope they also thought about how to use their past hardships to prepare for setting healthy boundaries and maximizing class time with their students. Sometimes the surface-level perfection hides the burnout smoldering within.

Creating habits of returning to your objectives and purpose for using a lesson or the way you organize your classroom will allow you to use your strengths as an educator. It will help you engage your students and ensure that you are helping them succeed when they're with you.

HACK 5

E: EXTEND YOUR REACH AND POSSIBILITIES
MAKE TIME FOR THE THINGS THAT
BRING YOU GROWTH AND JOY

Just because you're doing a lot more doesn't mean you're getting a lot more done. Don't confuse movement with progress.
— DENZEL WASHINGTON, ACTOR

THE PROBLEM: YOU'RE JUST GOING THROUGH THE MOTIONS AND FEEL YOU'RE TOO BUSY TO LEARN SOMETHING NEW AND TO DO WHAT YOU ENJOY

A STUDY CONDUCTED BY the University of Chicago reported that most Americans prefer to be busy instead of sitting still or having nothing to do. The study coined the term "idleness aversion," which suggests that we would rather be busy doing non-productive activities than doing the deep work required of us to achieve true growth. For example, by answering non-urgent emails, we can avoid the harder, deeper work that needs our attention.

Can you relate? Are you guilty of idleness aversion?

Think about it. When you run into people you haven't seen in a while, and they ask you how you are doing, what do you say? "Great! So busy!"

Although being busy isn't a bad thing, being busy for the sake of being busy becomes an excuse to keep us stuck in burnout. We may think about the new habits we must adopt, the people we need to distance ourselves from, and the solutions we must try—and it seems easier to assume "business as usual" and just get through the day. Or, you could move forward and out of burnout by taking the steps I've outlined, such as:

- Naming your burnout and stage

- Building your self-awareness

- Distancing yourself from tearer-downers (like the crabs in Hack 2)

- Seeking and finding solutions rather than problems

- Saying no to things you used to believe were non-negotiable

It takes work to get out of burnout, and no one can do it but you. Becoming an active participant in your life is the only way you can see growth out of burnout, and it's the only way to achieve BURNED-IN status. If you read this book but change nothing, you'll find yourself waking up each day and going through the motions of the life you've built for yourself at home and at school. We get up (is it 5:30 already?), rush out the door with a cup of coffee, listen to the same radio station in the car, say hi to the same people, go through the same lessons, face the same challenges, try to get work done after school, then jet out the door with the same bag full of papers to grade and projects to plan. It's the same routine at home before we crash into bed and wonder what we even accomplished all day. Just another day, another week ... just making it to winter break, or summer break, or retirement ... in twenty years.

Twenty years? That's a long time to "go through the motions." You want something new for yourself. Something different. Something that will help you reach new heights in your life.

If you've put Hacks 1 through 4 into practice, you should see yourself narrowing your focus, time, and energy, and opening up your possibilities for more joy in your life.

If you're feeling burned-out because you're going through the motions and not getting much out of life, you might find yourself searching for a way to stop spinning your tires, looking for opportunities to learn something new and break up the routine. But how? Where do you start?

In the following Hacks, you're going to learn how.

THE HACK: EXTEND YOUR REACH AND POSSIBILITIES

Up to this point, we've been focusing on what has led you to your current reality of burnout. Through reflection, soul-searching, and digging into your (perhaps not-so-distant) past, you now have a decent understanding of what caused you to burn out, how to handle or avoid those triggers, and who you want to be. Now it's time to take all of that work and your newfound understandings, pack them up, and move forward.

Though the previous Hacks may have prompted you to think about how you are currently spending your personal and professional time, we will take your self-exploration much further. Extending your reach and possibilities is all about what you're ready to bring into your life now and moving forward. We've been working from the inside out, and now it's time to focus on what we can bring in from the outside world.

It's easier and takes less effort to consume mindless content than to learn and apply personal growth strategies to our lives. No number of cute cat videos or science fiction books will supply the tools we need to create more happiness and fulfillment in our lives—but they're easy to access, and they make us laugh.

EXTENDING YOUR REACH AND POSSIBILITIES HAS MORE TO DO WITH ALLOWING YOURSELF THE SPACE TO THINK, DREAM, PLAN, AND CONNECT TO YOUR STRENGTHS AND ASPIRATIONS THAN IT DOES IN TRYING TO GET MORE DONE.

Consider Image 5.1. Imagine that the triangle is a representation of your time. Each corner represents how you may utilize your time: personal growth/joy, productivity, and busyness. If you placed a dot to show how you currently distribute your time (based on the activity lists you previously made), where would your dot be?

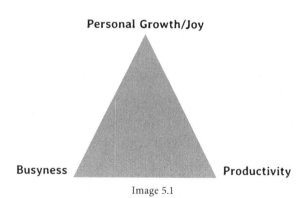

Image 5.1

My goal is for you to be able to place your dot between productivity and personal growth/joy. That is where you make time for the quiet rest and reflection you'll need if you want to move out of burnout.

By extending your reach and pushing yourself beyond your comfort zone, you keep yourself from settling for a mediocre existence where you are "just surviving" until retirement. By extending your reach, with the support of others and healthy habits, you allow yourself the ingredients you need to climb out of burnout and become a more well-rounded, fulfilled individual.

Extending your reach and possibilities is all about allowing for mindfulness instead of mindlessness, and I'm not talking about the stereotypical mindfulness practices of sitting cross-legged and reciting "om." Although meditation is a beautiful and powerful practice in growing our focus on the present moment, I'm also talking about connecting what you need to change about your beliefs, challenges, and daily habits to what you're reading, watching, and listening to daily. This practice will help you learn more about burnout, change your beliefs, build your brand, find solutions to your biggest challenges, and create a daily and weekly schedule that you can handle and enjoy.

I'm not telling you that you have to aspire to climb Mount Everest; prepare for your next job opportunity; pick up and move to another state; or consume multiple books, podcasts, and videos about self-help each day (unless you want to do those things). I am saying that for you to reach more balance between busyness, personal growth/joy, and productivity, you've got to start dedicating some of your downtimes to activities designed to help you learn, grow, and extend your possibilities. Choosing these activities will help you solve challenges and build habits into your life to help you grow.

Extending your reach and possibilities has more to do with allowing yourself the space to think, dream, plan, and connect with your strengths and aspirations than it does in trying to get more done. Consider how you're setting yourself up for success both in and out of your professional life. How are you ensuring that you can handle whatever life may throw at you next? What are you doing to keep your mind actively growing?

Assess your current possibilities and reach by asking yourself:

- What am I passionate about outside of school?

- What do I enjoy doing for leisure?

- What impact do I want to make on my world outside of school?

- Who do I want to hang out with the most outside of school?

Consider your answers and then ask:

- Do these things/people push me out of my comfort zone?

    - If so, what am I pushed to do or be?

    - Am I being pushed toward any of my short- or long-term goals?

    - Am I following through with what it takes to keep going and reach success?

- Am I making enough time to do these things and be with these people?

Ask yourself how you are extending your reach:

- What books am I reading?

- What podcasts do I listen to?

- What influencers do I follow?

- What YouTube videos inspire me?

- How often am I just quiet, doing nothing?

By asking these questions, you can move further along into a new burnout stage on your journey out of burnout altogether.

WHAT **YOU** CAN DO TOMORROW

You can control your schedule, instead of it controlling you. It may take time and focus, but you can and must do it if you want to ensure that you spend time on you and your growth out of burnout. You cannot grow into a happier, more fulfilled person without allowing yourself the time you need for such growth.

Look back on your Daily Habit Analysis and what your days and weeks currently look like, and decide what you want them to look like in the future. Then act.

- **Adopt a growth mindset.** In her book *Mindset*, Dr. Carol Dweck writes, "This growth mindset is based on the belief that your basic qualities are things you can cultivate through your efforts. Although people may differ in every which way—in their initial talents and aptitudes, interests, or temperaments— everyone can change and grow through application and experience." She goes on to say, "You have a choice. Mindsets are just beliefs. They're powerful beliefs, but they're just something in your mind, and you can change your mind."

Adopting a growth mindset is essential when it comes to reflecting on what brought you into burnout, your biggest challenges, and what you truly believe you can do about them. When you focus on what brings you joy and personal growth, you can extend your reach and expand your possibilities both personally and professionally.

- **Do your research.** It's not enough to know what brings you joy and what you want to become better at doing. You must put that desire into action and on your calendar. Google online courses, podcasts, or YouTube videos dedicated to helping you grow your knowledge and understanding. Make a plan for listening/watching each day, even for fifteen minutes.

   You can also research books and blogs dedicated to helping you grow. We live in a world filled with information by authors sharing their stories to help others (you) grow through what they've learned. Use these resources to draw out your path.

- **Call on your PLN for ideas.** The beauty behind a professional learning network is that it can include people who you see every day at work, people you've met on the internet, or a mixture of both.

They can extend your reach and possibilities because of the experiences *they* have with courses, podcasts, books, blogs, or videos that have helped them. Put a feeler out there and ask them what they recommend if you want to learn more about a topic.

A BLUEPRINT FOR FULL IMPLEMENTATION

If you currently spend your free time binging Netflix, watching hilarious YouTube videos, listening to entertaining books, and scrolling through social media, that's okay. But only if you're balancing that mindless escape with time to learn more about the possibilities you have in your one life.

STEP 1: Decide what brings you joy and what you want to learn.

Make a list of activities you would enjoy doing and would be interested in learning. These are your possibilities. Dream big and be honest with yourself.

STEP 2: Create a vision for how you will dedicate more time to these activities.

You either create your vision, or others will create it for you based on their needs. How many hours do you want to dedicate to work and to your life outside of work? Pick numbers.

There are 168 hours in a week and twenty-four in a day. We all know that, but let's break it down even further:

- If you have twenty-four hours in a day and spend eight of them sleeping (and you should be getting eight hours, because you need it and deserve it), you have sixteen hours a day to do life.

- That's your time allowance. Sixteen hours to spend as you choose.

That's right; I'm empowering you to believe that how you spend your time is a choice. You choose your profession; you choose what you say yes to; you choose where you live and how far away it is from your school. You choose it all. You also get to decide how you spend your time. How many hours a week do you want to dedicate to work. Fifty? Sixty? Forty-five? It's up to you.

Write that amount of time at the top of a piece of paper.

STEP 3: Budget your time.

Just like we budget money (at least I hope you do … think habits), we can budget our time. Let me show you how, and you can follow along in Image 5.2.

a. Using your paper with your time allowance number at the top, write the number of hours that you dream of working on school—and that's everything, including teaching, planning, prepping, grading, and even answering email. Let's say you want to work forty-five hours a week. (Don't laugh; it's possible.)

b. Now, under that write: M, T, W, Th, F, Sat, Sun.

c. You will see you have an allowance of sixteen hours a day, seven days a week, to choose how you spend

that forty-five hours on school, on whatever you
choose. I said it again: you choose what you spend it
on. Empowering, right?

Let's say you get up on Monday morning, work out, shower,
and get ready for your day. You get the kids breakfast, then they
play, watch TV, or get started on their eLearning as you open your
computer. It's 7:45.

From 7:45 to 9:45, you're answering emails, launching lessons,
and answering a few phone calls. Two hours. You just spent two
out of forty-five from your time allowance.

Only forty-three more hours of work to go.

You take a break to check on the kids, grab a snack, and get
back on the computer to plan and record some lessons, and before
you know it, another two hours have passed, and you've planned
and recorded your lessons for tomorrow.

Now, you've got to spend time helping your own kids with their
work, so you take an hour and a half to help them, grab lunch,
take a walk, and then dive back into work or a meeting with your
principal and a few teachers for forty-five minutes.

But tomorrow will look different because right away, you have a
collaboration meeting with four other teachers from 9 to 11, and
you're talking about plans for next year. So you're going to take
the morning to hang out with the kids and help them with their
work. Another two hours ...

As the week goes by, you realize that you may have to spend
time on Saturday checking work that has been turned in online.
No worries; you have budgeted three hours, and you will do it
from 8 to 11 on Saturday morning.

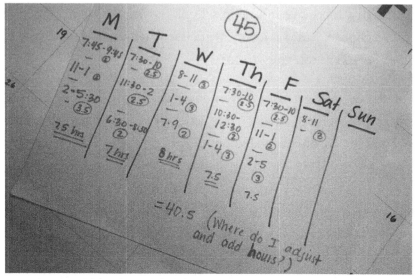

Image 5.2: This shows a scheduling example for a teacher in a fully virtual setting, but teachers in a classroom setting can apply the same ideas.

Budgeting how you spend your day will help you on your journey to creating more time for:

- Family and friends—if you're burned and unbalanced (or bored).

- Your side hustle, master's degree work, or course to learn a new skill you want to try in class—if you're burned and bored.

- Refiining your relationship-building skills, reading, listening, or watching digital content that will teach you what you can do to get over being over it—if you're burned and over it.

STEP 4: Dedicate yourself to discipline.

You've probably heard it said, "If you fail to plan, you plan to fail." Most teachers adhere to this in terms of lesson plans; however, we leave the rest of our lives to chance. Not anymore. Remember, you've now set boundaries, have better habits, and know how you want to extend your reach. It's time to plan for these things.

To do this, prioritize what is most important, batch similar tasks together, block the time in your calendar to get them done, and do them.

To get started, list all the high-priority tasks you have to do on a given day or week—and I'm talking about the actual tasks (grading, prepping, planning, and connecting with parents and students). From that list, batch them by highlighting those that belong together. See Image 5.3.

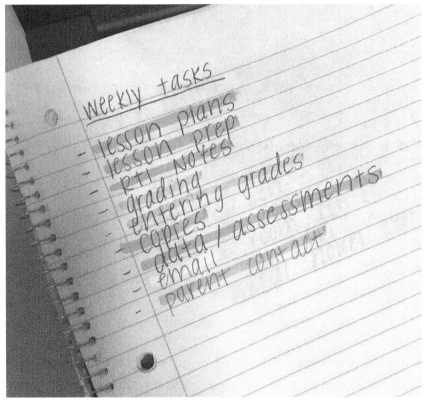

Image 5.3

Then, block time in your calendar, whether digital or manual, for each of these batches. It could look similar to Image 5.4.

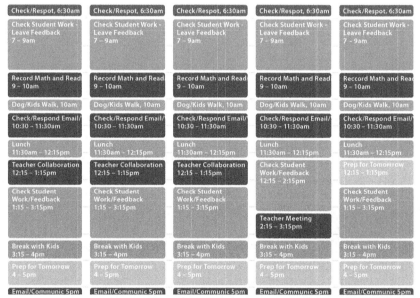

Image 5.4: This shows a calendar example for a teacher in a fully virtual setting, but you can apply the same time-blocking idea to a classroom setting.

STEP 5: Set your intention.

Before diving into each task, ask yourself:

- Am I doing this for the sake of being busy, or is this truly urgent and important to my students' success and my own?

- Can someone else do this?

- If I don't spend time on this, will anyone notice?

Then, set a timer for twenty-five minutes. State what you will focus on for that time. That is your one thing. That one thing is the only thing you're focusing on for twenty-five minutes. When your timer goes off, set it again for five minutes. Have a stretch, get a drink, go to the bathroom. Reflect on the progress you made and whether you need another twenty-five minutes for that one thing.

This is called a Pomodoro Technique. It was invented in the early 1990s by Francesco Cirillo, who named the system Pomodoro (Italian for tomato) after the tomato-shaped timer he used to track his work. The technique has become a popular way to intensely focus on one task at a time to get more done in less time.

OVERCOMING PUSHBACK

No matter what I do, I can't find time in my schedule to focus on things that interest me. Focus on two words here: "can't" and "find." Can't often is a euphemism for won't and (as you well know from working with students) can't also is the barrier that conveniently shows up in students' language when things are hard. Adults are often the same. Our brains want to save calories, so when things get hard, or we have to do something differently (ahem, habits and beliefs), we pretend like saying "I can't" gets us off the hook.

As for "find," you don't "find" time, you "make" it. You will make time for things that matter to you and your growth. If not, you will make excuses (i.e., "I can't because ..." insert Excuse Edward here).

I don't know what I want. I'm so used to being exhausted and consumed with work. Now that I have more time, I don't know my passions or what I enjoy. Believe it or not, this is a good thing because you're now able to open up possibilities for new beliefs and habits. This is why it's critical to internalize and act on Hacks 1 through 4 before you reach this point. You now know more about yourself and can use the time you have for

133

self-discovery and new habit-forming practices that will allow you to grow continually.

If I'm not busy, then I'm lazy. That is a lie you're telling yourself because our cultural norm is to be 100 percent booked. When we wear our busyness and exhaustion as a badge of honor, we may find ourselves humble-bragging about how much work we've done for the PTO Cookie Drive or how exhausted we are from staying up until 2 a.m. gluing googly eyes on paper plates for our students' Grandparents' Day project. Our choice? Yes. Necessary? I'll let you answer that.

Just as I described in Hack 2, you get to choose how you talk to yourself. In Hack 3, I encouraged you to pay attention to the way you view your reality. You get to decide on the truth.

THE HACK IN ACTION
By Holly T., school librarian

I had been reading professional development books to become a better teacher, but once I read a personal development book to become a better me, I was hooked. From then on, I kept my "background noise" stocked with podcasts and audiobooks. Day after day, commute after commute, piles of laundry and washed floors later, I was filling my soul with words and ideas that began to transform my thinking. I had been spending so much time controlling my actions, but in reality, when I slowed down and worked on my thoughts, the actions became easier.

My best examples are when I read books on time management that gave me the reasons why to-do lists only go so far and shared new perspectives on how I spend my free time. After reading *The Miracle Morning* by Hal Elrod, I realized that if I woke up about thirty minutes before my family, I would be a happier, more awake mom than when my kids pulled me out of sleep. It also helped me learn how doing my thirty-minute workout at the start of my day would completely change my outlook for tackling the rest of the day. I knew I had done something hard in the first hour of waking up, and so I knew I could conquer other hard things during the day. This was also the catalyst for helping me learn how to batch work and block my time in the library so I could feel more focused and get more done in less time. I started to turn to books, blogs, and podcasts to help me feel better about tough (really tough) situations. In the past, I might turn to a glass of wine and an indulgent TV show, but those "comforts" didn't fix my soul. When the wine was gone, the feelings and problems were still there, just magnified with the guilt of drinking them away. I would get in an argument with my husband and turn to a blog post about marriage from my favorite mom podcast, called Coffee + Crumbs. The women told stories that mirrored mine and often described how they resolved arguments and continued in their happy marriages. I didn't feel alone.

After a hard day at school, I often found a teaching podcast that explained how a teacher got through a tough time or used specific strategies to solve a problem. I didn't feel like a failure.

I found out I was going to need a serious surgery, and I read a book to help calm my anxiety and give me the tools to manage my feelings. Reading *The Universe Has Your Back* by Gabrielle Bernstein made me feel connected.

When I lost a close friend to cancer, books taught me how to help others deal with grief while I wrestled with my own. They also told me it was okay to laugh. I felt like I had a team of experts helping me.

I keep finding books that give me the language for my feelings and thoughts. Because when I understand and have the confidence to rise from negative and crushing feelings and thoughts, I am simply more productive, happier, and a better teacher, mom, wife, and friend. As the school librarian, I have always believed that there is magic in books, but only since reading personal development books have I been able to work that magic seamlessly into every part of my life.

Burnout is an opportunity to grow and make phenomenal changes in your life. You have two choices when you hit rock bottom: you can go up or stay down. Although it may be easier to stay at rock bottom because you don't have to do anything hard, scary, or different, chances are it may be just as challenging to remain there unhappy, alone, and isolated.

If you look at burnout as an opportunity to change your life, take risks, and advocate for yourself and others like you, you can grow personally and professionally. The beauty is that it's your choice. The second you choose to take action—even though it's hard—you will be better able to tackle any hardship or crisis because you know you're becoming a more empowered teacher and person.

HACK 6

D: DETERMINE YOUR LONG-TERM GOALS
CREATE A VISION FOR WHERE YOU WANT TO GO

*Setting goals is the first step in turning
the invisible into the visible.*

— TONY ROBBINS, MOTIVATIONAL COACH

THE PROBLEM: YOU AREN'T HAPPY WHERE YOU ARE OR WITH HOW THINGS ARE GOING—BUT YOU DON'T KNOW WHAT YOU WANT OR HOW TO CHANGE THINGS

WHEN I WAS a senior in high school, I got pregnant with my oldest daughter. At the time, my boyfriend (now my husband) was a freshman at Purdue University. Everyone asked us, "What are you going to do?" Although we knew the road would be challenging, we knew we wanted to continue with our plans to go to college and get degrees. We wanted to give our daughter a life filled with stability, fun, and success.

We decided he would move home after finishing his freshman year, and we would both go to college in Fort Wayne, close to where we now live. We sat down and mapped out our plan. We didn't know all the answers or exactly how we were going to make it happen, but we documented where we wanted to be in three, five, and ten years. Our daughter was born on August 3, 2001, two months after my high school graduation. Five years later, in December of 2006, I graduated with my bachelor's in education, and my husband had already been hired for his first teaching job.

We didn't get lucky. No one else supported us financially. But we had a vision and goals, and through the ups and downs, we supported one another. No excuses. Along that journey, we had to work around unexpected roadblocks and steep climbs, but we did it, and it all started with a vision and goals. And a lot of planning and re-planning.

That's what this Hack is all about: setting goals and making things happen. No matter what roadblock or crisis you face, you can tap into the power of setting goals and planning, defining your future, and continuing to focus forward when times are tough.

As a teacher struggling with burnout, you must have a strong desire to change your life, and a strong plan of action. We deal with constant change and challenge, and when you can look through those things and continue to focus on your goals, your plan, and your daily discipline and intention, you'll know you're on the right path out of your burnout type and stage.

THE HACK: DETERMINE YOUR LONG-TERM GOALS

What goals have you set for yourself? Read the following questions, and then sit back, close your eyes, and think about your answers.

- What goals did you set when you were younger (when you were in middle school, let's say)?

- What goals did you set for yourself when you were graduating high school?

- What goals did you set when you were graduating college?

- How about now? What goals have you set for yourself recently?

Do your current goals sound like this:

- "My goal is to make it through the week."

- "If I can get to Christmas break, I'll be good."

- "Once this quarantine is over, I'll be happy again. Wait ... was I happy?"

- "I just have to make it through the day, then I can get out of here."

- "I'm just holding out for retirement in fifteen years."

Fifteen years? Are you kidding me? Think of all the possibilities for change and growth you're missing by being in survival mode for that long. This, my friend, is no way to live a life. Not now. Not ever. And if you've been living this way, the time for change is now.

Why is it essential for us to continue to set long-term goals? Because setting goals:

- Pushes us ahead and gives us a path to follow

- Turns huge mountains into walkable, rolling hills

- Helps us believe in ourselves and our possibilities (ahem … remember Hack 5?)

- Keeps us focused on what we truly want

- Helps us live the happiest, most fulfilled life possible

- Holds us accountable when we fail

Have you stopped setting goals because you're afraid to fail? In *Mindset*, Carol Dweck addresses the topic of failure in the book's "Defining Moments" section. She writes, "Even in the growth mindset, failure can be a painful experience. But it doesn't define you. It's a problem to be faced, dealt with, and learned from."

BURNOUT IS A CALL FOR CHANGE AND OFFERS US A HUGE OPPORTUNITY TO DO SOMETHING DIFFERENT.

If you have set goals for yourself in the past and failed, good! What did you learn? Maybe the goal was too deep or too broad? No problem. We'll address it in the next Hack. However, perhaps the problem was that you didn't have anyone to talk to and support you through your goal mastery.

Everyone needs support when tackling a goal, so don't attempt to go it alone. Call on your burnout buddy to help you set, break down, and achieve your goals.

Recall that in Hack 5, I asked you how you were extending your reach. So, what's changed? Have you put anything into motion? If not, you need to back up, reread, and reflect, because without doing that work, this step won't be as attainable. Are you ready? Great. Let's burn on!

WHAT YOU CAN DO TOMORROW

- **Write it out.** If it's been a while since you've thought about what you want from your life and career, grab a pencil, paper, and favorite beverage. Then dream. You may be an adult with multiple responsibilities, but that doesn't mean you can't do big things for yourself, your family, and your career. Write them down. Imagine how you would feel if you achieved these dreams.

- **Repeat what you want, say it out loud, and pretend you've already achieved it.** It doesn't matter whether you call it autosuggestion or manifestation. What matters is that you know what you want, and you keep that desire at the forefront of your mind. Every day. In his book *Think and Grow Rich*, Napoleon Hill writes, "Your ability to use the principle of autosuggestion will depend, very largely, upon your capacity to concentrate upon a given desire until that desire becomes a burning obsession."

  When we allow ourselves to "relax" by watching trashy Netflix specials or funny videos on YouTube or TikTok, we're distracting our minds and allowing ourselves to choose mindlessness over mindfulness. If you're mindful of what you want, you focus on it over and over again.

Write what you want every morning, say it out loud, talk about it like it's already happened, and write it out again before you go to bed. You'll be amazed at how this works.

- **Show gratitude.** One of the most significant ways to open your mind and heart to get what you want is to be grateful for what you already have. Being thankful for a roof over your head (even though it may not be the home you want in five years), your current job (although it may not be at your school of choice), and your health (even if you want to lose twenty pounds) are ways to help you realize how lucky you are to wake up each day and have the ability to dream bigger dreams for yourself.

  You can also show gratitude for your burnout. Burnout is a call for change and offers us a huge opportunity to do something different so we can grow and share our story with others who are hurting. Being grateful for your burnout means you're looking at challenges and changes as a way to test your strengths and habits to see if you've become strong enough to serve, lead, and practice in a new way.

- **Create or find a mastermind.** As teachers, we're more than familiar with collaboration. However, we also know that collaboration today is often a forced meeting with a specific agenda with people who are different from one another and have different beliefs about how they teach and assess learning.

On the other hand, a mastermind is a small group of people with similar goals and beliefs and a determination to reach their goals while gaining knowledge and giving and receiving accountability to take consistent and intentional actions toward those goals.

You can create a mastermind by merely sending out an email, Facebook message, or social media post stating your goals, asking if anyone has similar goals, and if they want to join a group of people who desire to keep each other accountable.

A BLUEPRINT FOR FULL IMPLEMENTATION

These steps to determine what you want out of life are a mixture of practices I've learned through research, podcasts, books, and my own experiences. You don't have to do this with fidelity or rigidity. Do this your way, in your style. The best part is that your goals belong to you—and so does your process for discovering them. Think of these steps as a guideline and add your own twist. You have full autonomy to be creative and dream big.

STEP 1: Big Dreams Brain Dump: what do you want for yourself? Dream big!

This step is self-explanatory. You simply set a timer for five minutes and dump all your biggest dreams (personal and professional) onto a journal or a piece of paper or a digital document. Just lay it all out there. Think one year, three years, and five years into the future. Don't hold back. Are you afraid to add anything? Don't be. This is a safe space. This is *your* space.

After you finish this list, you can see what you truly want. In writing. All there, right in front of you. Read the list out loud (maybe even shout it). Own that list.

STEP 2: Check-in: what's gone well in the last year?

On the next page, do another brain dump. What are you pleased about from the last year? What went well? What makes you smile? What happened that made you feel accomplished or brought you joy, both personal and professional?

STEP 3: Check-in: what *hasn't* gone well in the last year?

Okay, these are probably things you're stuck thinking about all the time anyway; otherwise, you wouldn't be here. Slap those puppies in your journal or paper or computer. Get them out of your brain and in front of your eyeballs. It's an ideal time to revisit your "challenges" list from Hack 3, and include them here too. The goal is to look at this list and decide what you're going to take action on.

STEP 4: Heck yes: what will you say yes to in the coming year?

Now we're planning ahead. You're deciding what you will stand for this coming year, starting right now. There's no waiting for January 1. You're an action-taker, so go ahead … set a timer for another five minutes and think of all the things you're going to say yes to.

STEP 5: Heck no: what will you say no to in the coming year?

We had this conversation back in Hack 5, and although we can't say "no, thanks" to everything asked of us, we can say, "not right now" to others. So what are they? What will you stand against in the coming year? Don't be afraid; you can make a plan to let go gradually.

STEP 6: Professional goals: what do you want for yourself in the next one, three, and five years?

You may have already written these in your Big Dreams Brain Dump, and that's fine. Just write down the professional goals here, so we can use them in Hack 7 as we initiate lasting change. Remember, think gradual and with guided flexibility. You won't limit yourself if you find in six months that you didn't dream big enough. You'll be surprised what a little action and willpower can do for your career. Ready, set your timer, go!

STEP 7: Personal goals: what do you want for yourself in the next one, three, and five years?

Go ahead and dream big again. When I started this journey, one of my biggest personal goals was moving out of our hometown to a nearby city that we loved. It seemed daunting and scary at the time, considering we'd dumped a bunch of money into our country house, but we still talk about our great decision to move, and that was years ago.

It's time for you to take action in your personal life, so set your timer for five minutes.

STEP 8: Develop a Word of the Year.

You can sleep on this, but not without doing a little digging first. Here are the steps to follow before you step away to chew on this.

1. Go back through all your brain dumping and add, delete, and edit your answers. In your excitement, you may have forgotten items.

2. Get a highlighter and look for words that repeat or are synonymous with other words. Highlight those words.

3. Write out the words that repeat or are similar, and that's where your Word of the Year will be born. Think about the words, try them on, and see what feels right as the one top word that best summarizes your intentions for the year.

4. As promised, take a break from this and go for a walk or take a nap or whatever you want while you mull over your options.

5. Choose your word and make sure you can commit to it. Write your Word of the Year on a piece of clean paper and, if you're into this, decorate it any way you'd like. Add favorite colors or designs. You can also do this same exercise digitally.

STEP 9: Reassess your goals and make sure they're SMART.

One day in 2016, I sat at a McDonald's with a friend, and we talked about how to change our lives. I had been feeling lost (again). I had taken action in my life, and yet I still felt like everything was crumpled up or broken at my feet.

As she and I dreamed about what our futures would look like a year or two from that day, she mentioned SMART goals, which were new to me. If you aren't familiar with SMART goals, let me help you understand how to use them within the educational context, with the scenario of a teacher who set a goal to get a master's degree. That teacher can go through the SMART acronym, as follows:

S: Specific (what, why, and how): "My goal is to decide what master's degree program I want to pursue because I know that I don't want to continue to be in the classroom, but I want to keep working with teachers and students."

M: Measurable (long-term/short-term): "I will research x types of degrees by x date to determine what I want to get my master's degree in and to graduate by x date. If I don't find the thing that feels right, I may need to change my goal." (Side note: You may have an end date for the entire goal, and dates that lead you to that main goal to keep you on track.)

A: Achievable (agreed, attainable): "I'm going to look for a degree program that I can visualize myself doing and enjoying. My family knows about my goals and are supportive of them."

R: Relevant (measure outcomes, not activities): "After all the research, I will decide which degree program will best fit my personality, and I will decide how much time I want to spend on the degree so I won't quit."

T: Time-Bound (time-limited, time-sensitive): "I'll choose what degree I want to pursue by x date so that I have time to fill out my application and make plans for myself and my family as I work toward reaching this goal."

These steps may seem overwhelming at first glance. However, you can complete this Hack in a little over an hour if you take advice from Hack 5 and make time for this step, which will offer you clarity and definite desire—which you need in order to define and stick to goals that will propel you forward on your journey out of burnout.

OVERCOMING PUSHBACK

I'm too old to set big goals for myself. If that's what you say to yourself, then it will be the truth. Your reality starts with your beliefs, and whatever you believe will be proven true by your reticular activating system. If you believe it to be true, your brain will look for ways to prove it. The real truth is that you are never too old to change your reality. Believe that, and you can start taking action today.

Others will judge me, think I'm crazy, and laugh at me if I talk about things like they've already happened or share my dreams. Then you're sharing your dreams with the wrong people. Remember the story about the crabs when I laid out the difference between tearer-downers and builder-uppers? Have you stopped to think about who you're hanging out with the most and whether they are keeping you where you are or pushing you to move forward with what you truly want for yourself?

I want to leave education, but I don't have any other skills. Being an empowered teacher who takes daily action to avoid burnout and helps others do the same doesn't mean you have to remain a teacher in the classroom or district where you currently work. If you're miserable and don't want to be in the classroom, you aren't doing anyone any favors. Your students, colleagues, and administrators likely know you don't want to be there too. Teachers carry multiple skill sets they can use in many other career fields. You're an excellent communicator, curriculum planner, project manager, mediator, organizer, and more. Of course, make sure you're in good shape financially and allow yourself time to find a job where you can thrive while fulfilling your financial needs and goals. If it's not teaching where you are or teaching at all, it is your life and your choice to go in a different direction.

THE HACK IN ACTION
By Sabrina M., technology integrationist

I had been struggling with my job and administration, which were causing lots of stress. I was feeling unappreciated and disrespected and had lost my enthusiasm for my job. I wanted to be happy at work again.

First, I listed what had changed, what had gone well, and what had not gone well. I had experienced changes in my job expectations, administration, my attitude, and just feeling burned-out. I took the Teacher Burnout quiz and learned that I am a hybrid of teacher burnout types, and I was given strategies to help me change my mindset from negative to positive. During the "Teacher Brand" activity, we were to find out how others perceived us, so I sent out a survey asking my colleagues to list four words they thought of when they heard my name. This activity was not within my comfort zone and took bravery on my part. I got affirming responses. One response, however, changed how I viewed myself and my unhappiness. It said: *mean and demanding.* Wait—that wasn't me … or was it?

Even though it was only one person's opinion, I made it a goal to put myself out there more. I ate lunch with other teachers in the lounge more often. I asked them how they were doing and paid more attention to their needs. As a tech coach, I wanted to be approachable and positive, so I began to become an involved part of the community. I had alienated myself, leading to my negative mindset, which fueled my unhappiness. Another exercise was choosing our Word of the Year. I chose "release." It had a double meaning. I would release the negative thoughts (anger, resentment, feeling underappreciated) from my mind and replace them with more energetic and positive thoughts that I would release (staying focused, practicing self-care, and being grateful). I ordered jewelry with my "word" engraved as a reminder of my choice.

I came to realize that yes, it is a choice. It helped me stay focused on self-improvement and what truly mattered. I developed a plan of action that helped me change the way I thought. I took steps to show more gratitude for my job, family, and friends. It also reminded me not to worry about things I can't control, but instead focus on what I can control. A few trusted colleagues let me know when my attitude was slipping. I found it helpful to have this support to keep me grounded and on track.

What mattered to me was doing what was best for my students, so I focused on my classes and not the "other stuff." By taking advice and guidance, I accomplished one of my professional goals, which was to become Google Certified. This gave me a feeling of credibility and accomplishment. For my personal goal, I focused on self-care and continued positivity and gratitude. I have seen a marked improvement in my mindset, and as a result, I have been much happier. I don't let things stress me out as much, and I am so grateful for the BURNED-IN Teacher group support.

Setting goals is not a habit to revisit one time a year. We can continually think about our progress toward our high priorities and the activities that are vital to our growth and happiness.

Setting goals means you're striving to do and be what is best for you and those you serve. Your goals can be about bringing more simplicity into your life, saying no more often, or taking steps to get that job you've always wanted. You can also share your goals with the ones you love and care about the most, uniting you on a new level and bringing you closer together.

What are your goals? How are you going to use them to get you out of burnout?

HACK 7

I: INITIATE LASTING CHANGE
BUILD SELF-DISCIPLINE TO TAKE INTENTIONAL MONTHLY, WEEKLY, AND DAILY ACTION

A goal without a plan is just a wish.
— ANTOINE DE SAINT-EXUPÉRY, WRITER

THE PROBLEM: YOU DON'T KNOW HOW TO TAKE ACTION TOWARD YOUR GOALS

IT'S NO SHOCK that teachers are overwhelmed. As educators, we wear many hats and perform many professions all rolled into one. We're nurses, counselors, project managers, salespersons, mediators, scientists, and so many others. In addition to being teachers, we're partners, parents, siblings, sons, and daughters who have dreams, goals, and hobbies.

Because of these many roles, I've witnessed teachers, friends, and myself struggle inside of burnout. When we set big goals and aspirations and then decide to take action, hardship happens, and we end up throwing in the towel. Our difficulties may include gaining new students who challenge our original goals, getting an illness that takes us out of commission, realizing the new principal has new initiatives, and experiencing a global pandemic. The possibilities are endless for challenges and changes in our daily lives, but our desire to get out and stay out of burnout has to be so defined and actionable that nothing can rock us.

Just setting goals and having the best intentions won't get us where we want to go as teachers or in our lives outside of teaching. After defining your personal and professional goals in Hack 6, you may find yourself saying, "Now what?" You may be wondering how on earth you can make the time for the action you need to take to bring your goals into reality.

Your habit of "just making it through the day and week" could be overtaking your belief that you *can* make the time for positive action.

I used to let things creep up on me. I considered possibilities but didn't plan for anything. No calendar, no journal, no goals … just going through the motions and allowing other people's plans to happen to me. Can you relate? Or do you practice journaling, planning, and reflecting daily? We aren't talking about lesson planning here.

As Aesop said, "Slow and steady wins the race." It seems so counterintuitive to slow down, get quiet, and think, doesn't it? Who has time for that? But think back to Hack 5, where we learned not to be busy just for the sake of being busy. We need to stop the busyness so we can jump into being more focused on ourselves, our reach, possibilities, and goals. That means slowing down and focusing on the meaning of being productive.

If you aren't journaling, listing, and reflecting on your goals and dreams consistently, then you're keeping it all in your head, jumbled up and cluttered. If you aren't taking the time to get your thoughts out of your brain and neatly placing them somewhere else, then overwhelm and the consumption of work, parenting, and living will continue to consume you. (You may want to write in *Permission to Pause: A Journal for Teachers* by Dorothy VanderJagt, also published by Times 10 Publications.)

If you don't know where to start, Overwhelm Olivia is in your head, and you're stuck again, it's time to bring Step-by-Step Sabrina on board. She will help you focus on the most crucial changes that will impact your vision. Whether your goal is to make home-cooked meals for your family to eat together two nights a week, to go on a walk with your partner four days a week, or to sell your home and move to a town that is closer to school, you must make it a priority to take the steps to reach those goals.

THE HACK: INITIATE LASTING CHANGE

Planning for change is the fun part. Now we're going to plan for the harder part: initiating lasting change through monthly, weekly, and daily planning. It's a great time to do your brain dumping and planning for your future that I walked you through in Hack 6. Remember, if you fail to plan, you plan to fail. I'm here and ready when you are.

Beating burnout requires you to be an active participant in your life; therefore, putting you in the driver's seat in the same car where you used to be a passenger in the backseat. And, just like a vehicle's driver, you must know your destination (your goals) and have a plan for how to get there (your directions), as well as a reason for going (your purpose).

The goal of this Hack is to help you initiate lasting change by developing healthy habits of reflection, planning, and action-taking on your journey out of burnout. Through writing, listing, and focusing on what is most important to you, you can start your action steps in the right direction.

If you haven't already, now is the time to find or purchase a notebook as your roadmap to your goals. You're going to take intentional weekly and daily action through brain dumping, planning, and implementing, and you can't keep all of this work in your head. Journaling and reflection can help eliminate overwhelm, create clarity, generate focus, and initiate lasting change.

YOU ARE THE BOSS AND CREATOR OF YOUR FUTURE.

To prepare for crisis, hardship, and the challenges of life, we have to include daily practices that help us eliminate the stress, overwhelm, and lack of balance.

Journaling and planning are more than "woo-woo" rituals that poets and monks do every day as the sun rises and birds and butterflies circle above them. You can journal in a practical way for the sake of initiating lasting change. Your journal entries can serve as a brain dump, to-do list, reflection, and accountability check—all in one.

WHAT YOU CAN DO TOMORROW

- **Buy a paper planner or use Google Calendar.** It may seem old-school, but a paper planner is a great place to dump goal dates and check-ins with pencil, and then reschedule as needed. My favorite planner was a $6 planner from Kroger with a monthly calendar and weekly planner where I could do my brain dumping and planning and then transfer hard dates to my Google Calendar. Using sub-calendars and color-coding (you can take the teacher out of the classroom, but never the classroom out of the teacher), I created time blocks and batches that I live by each day. Having a safe and consistent place to dream big and see my dream dates on a calendar has changed my life, and I don't know how I accomplished anything until I discovered this planner trick at age thirty-three.

- **Plan time to check in weekly with your mastermind, accountability partner, or burnout buddy.** It's hard to create new habits. Doing it alone is even harder. Taking time to check in with someone who builds you up and helps keep you accountable is crucial to your success in getting out of burnout. When you connect with them for an intentional conversation, set up the structure to focus on your progress, your wins, and your next steps. Don't spend too much time focusing on the hardships. Your continued focus on you and your progress will keep you moving forward.

- **Utilize backward design to break down your goals.** Stephen Covey described backward design as beginning with the end in mind. It means thinking about your destination and then planning small steps for how you will get there.

According to *The Glossary of Education Reform*, "Backward design ... is a process that educators use to design learning experiences and instructional techniques to achieve specific learning goals. Backward design begins with the objectives of a unit or course—what students are expected to learn and be able to do—and then proceeds backward to create lessons that achieve those desired goals."

It's a great practice for planning lessons and units of study, but it's also a smart way to plan for our success. That's why I've incorporated backward design into my daily journaling practice, and I'm sharing it with you.

I'm also going to walk you through how to bring backward design into your everyday life to help you initiate the lasting change you so desperately want and need.

A successful backward design journal will:

- Start with the main goal (from your personal or professional goals lists).

- Consider the action steps you need to take to get there.

- Break the action steps into smaller tasks that you can complete during your days and weeks (to make the goal more attainable).

Burnout comes from feeling that you have to achieve all goals, lists, and tasks in your life at the same time. Take a deep breath, set your priorities, and take small actions toward your goals one month, week, and day at a time.

- **Create a vision/mission board.** It's time to get your dreams out of your head and into reality. All of the work you've done so far in Hacks 1 through 6 needs to be physically (or digitally) put out there. It's no time to be shy; however, you don't have to show your beliefs, goals, and dreams to everyone. Having a few people on your support team is a key ingredient to a successful victory over burnout.

    You are the boss and creator of your future. Therefore, you get to choose who comes into contact with your vision/mission board.

    Let your creative juices flow. You may want to create a digital board, such as the one I created with Google Slides and set as my screensaver. You can create a secret Pinterest board or get crafty with poster board, glue, scissors, tape, and paint. The point is to build a board to display your dreams and goals.

    On your board, include:

- Your Word of the Year
- Your people
- Your core values
- Your aspirations of a happier, more fulfilled life as a teacher (or images that represent them)
- The things you will say yes to (or representative images)
- Your personal and professional goals (or representative images)

- **Decide what you will adopt, change, or abandon.** If you keep doing the same things, you'll keep getting the same results. Several people have been credited with this quote that drives home the point: "Insanity is doing the same thing over and over again and expecting different results."

  To achieve the dreams on your vision/mission board, you cannot continue to do, say, feel, or believe the same things you did before reading this book. So ...

  What are you going to adopt in your life? Might I suggest:

  - More positive people
  - A supportive group and/or professional learning network
  - Lessons from heroes and mentors

- Core values, a personal mission statement, and a teacher brand
- A healthier work/life balance

What changes will you make today? No need to wait to start changing until one, three, or five years from now. Start changing now to achieve mastery of your one-, three-, and five-year goals. Consider changing your:

- People you hang out with the most
- Schedule
- Priorities
- Openness to seeking support
- Core values
- Personal mission statement
- Teacher brand

What are you willing to let go? Often, we aren't ready to let go of what holds us back the most. So think hard about your current practices, habits, and mental state, and whether or not they serve your core values, personal mission statement, and brand. Ultimately, do they serve your long- and short-term goals?

- Do you have bad habits you need to lose?
- Do you have a negative mentality you need to abandon?

- Do you have toxic people in your life who you need to distance yourself from?
- Do you need to rid yourself of the fear of being vulnerable?

A BLUEPRINT FOR FULL IMPLEMENTATION

STEP 1: Start with a monthly or quarterly goal-setting session.

Using the practices in Hack 6, set aside time each month (using a calendar reminder) to go through the BURNED-IN process, reassess your goals, and readjust your steps.

Page 1: Prioritize your personal goals and number them (you can change the priority at any time).

Page 2: Prioritize your professional goals and number them.

Page 3: Select your number-one personal goal and write it down (this will be your personal goal to focus on for the next one to three months). Use what we learned about SMART goals to break it down.

Page 4: List the action steps you'll need to follow with guided flexibility to achieve each goal.

Page 5: Make a list of smaller tasks to complete the steps.

*Repeat this either on the last day of each month, or the first. It's up to you. Put a reminder in your calendar to get this done. You'll be surprised at how much focus this creates.

STEP 2: Make time each week for a weekly check-in with yourself.

Do this practice every Sunday night to help you sleep better the night before your week begins.

1. Title your document "Weekly Planning Brain Dump" and add subtitles for your Three-Month Personal Goals and Three-Month Professional Goals.

2. Below each, write down what tasks you're going to do that week to reach your three-month goals.

3. Make a list of personal and professional events coming up that week.

4. On the next blank page or in your preferred planner or calendar, list out each item you will strive to complete each day, Monday through Friday.

The real power behind this practice comes when you can look back at the progress you've made along your journey.

STEP 3: Set aside a few minutes each day to review your plan and progress.

1. Each morning, start a new blank page and date it.

2. Write out "Professional Goals" and "Personal Goals" at the top, and if you'd like, add your Word of the Year.

3. Write:

   • Three things you're grateful for.

   • Two things you're going to check off your task list (from your monthly or weekly journal) today.

   • One affirmation or quote you're going to focus on throughout the day (this could be an Agent of Change).

4. Close your eyes, take a deep breath, and envision an ideal day. Expect challenges and times when things won't go your way. Breathe out your tension, worry, and anxiety.

5. State your affirmation.

6. Leave space at the bottom.

7. ~~Your Day Happens Here~~

8. Each night, go back to your page from the morning.

9. Reread your morning gratitude and goals.

10. At the bottom, record:
   - What went well?
   - What could have been better?

11. Close your eyes. Take a deep breath and be grateful for another day. Smile. You're taking big leaps in your life with these small steps each day.

12. Say, "Tomorrow is another day for me to try again," or use another statement that puts you in control of you. Again, do what works best for you. The important thing is to start something and be consistent in whatever you choose to adopt or create. The alternative is to leave all of those dreams, goals, and tasks in your head. If you stay foggy, you'll be doomed to become overwhelmed, unfocused, and unmotivated again. But if you stay focused on moving forward, you will move out of burnout.

You will feel like shouting, "I'm doing it! I'm initiating lasting change. I'm now taking daily steps toward a happier and more fulfilled me. I did this." Pat yourself on the back, grab your favorite drink, and toast to your success.

OVERCOMING PUSHBACK

I've tried journaling and planning before. It doesn't work for me. The importance of this practice doesn't depend on you doing this exactly the way I've outlined it. Rather, it is in you deciding your highest personal and professional priority, breaking it down into actionable steps, and then placing those steps into your weeks and days with intention. Making your goals and action steps visible and putting them on a calendar creates a measuring stick for your progress. As the saying goes, "What gets measured gets managed." The more you make a conscious effort to track when you'll take action, the more you will see measured progress and see where you resist progress.

I need a fancy, cute planner so I can post my planner on Instagram. Unless you're motivated by cute planners, all you truly need is a spiral notebook, paper planner, or Google Calendar. I've even ripped used pages out of our daughters' lightly used school notebooks and used the remaining pages. Nothing fancy needed here, just discipline and intention to keep moving forward in small, imperfect steps toward what makes you happier and more fulfilled.

I always start initiatives like this, and then I quit. Quitting is a habit, and habits are hard to break. Try this: when you feel like quitting, commit to two minutes. That's it. For example, when you don't want to do something, like your weekly brain dump, simply set your timer for two minutes and get started. Starting is the hardest part, so after two minutes, you may find that you're in the flow and you want to keep going. If you still don't feel like continuing, it's okay to take a break from it.

Quitting can be a good thing. Author Seth Godin wrote, "Winners quit all the time. They just quit the right stuff at the right time." So if your past efforts have led you to quit, my question for you is, "Why did you quit?" Quitting is a sign of disconnection between you and your why, so if what you were making an effort toward wasn't aligned with your core values, or if you hadn't set specific goals, you quit.

Quitting is also a good thing when it comes to bad habits, tearer-downers, and past teaching and time-management practices that didn't serve you or your students.

THE HACK IN ACTION
By Jennifer S., classroom teacher

At the start of 2016, I was overwhelmed in every possible area of my life. I struggled to find the joy in my teaching, my house was full of stuff we didn't need, and I was uncomfortable with my weight. My work-work-life balance as a teacher, family photographer, wife, and mother of three was unbalanced, or more accurate, nonexistent. I didn't want to go to work anymore because I felt unappreciated and disconnected from my students and colleagues. While a small part of that may have had to do with my actual situation at work, I knew that most of it had to do with my management, or lack thereof, of my life in general.

I decided that maybe setting goals would be a good idea, but I had done that before, even written them down, and never got anywhere with them. This time, a few things were going to be different, and I had big reasons why. First, I had hit a low low, and it was finally apparent to me how depressed I was. Second, I set a meeting with a friend to discuss and share our goals for the year, so I knew I would have to take the time to think deeply before heading into that conversation. And finally, I bought a nice leather (well, possibly pleather) notebook that I loved. You don't need a lovely notebook, but I knew if I loved it, I would want to write in it more. I have my students decorate their writer's notebooks each year to help make them into special places that they truly want to delve into every day, so I applied that same idea to my writing, and honestly, it helped.

When I started, I wrote down every possible goal, big or small, that I wanted to accomplish that year. I had nine goals, and once I started writing, those goals were incredibly clear, which made me realize how important they each were and how ready I was to make lasting changes in my life. After writing the list of goals on the first page, I wrote each one at the top of a separate page, spaced a few pages apart. Then on each of those pages, underneath the goal, I wrote my "why" for that goal. Every goal had more than one reason why I wanted to reach it, and I spent quite a few days writing these down and coming back to them and adding to them. I even added more reasons throughout the year as I revisited my goals. I tried to dig deep for those reasons; I was brutally honest about why things needed to change and why each goal was critical for my personal and professional health. I realized early on that every goal was connected to the others in ways I hadn't noticed before writing them down. Everything came back around to wanting to simplify, organize, and maintain areas of my life that I currently had allowed to go completely awry. So instead of one word for the year, I had three: Simplify. Organize. Maintain.

After flushing out every big and small reason I wanted to

accomplish each goal, I turned the page and began my list of "how" for each goal. It was a messy list, rarely in any kind of order, but it was a list of actionable small steps I could take. In making this list, I asked myself more questions, like how I was going to reach that goal, what steps I had to take to get started, if I needed materials or resources, and how often I needed to do certain actionable items. For some goals, I made a list of to-do items or a chart with dates by which to accomplish mini-goals. Again, I added ideas to these lists throughout the year and even crossed out items as I accomplished them.

After all of this, I met with my friend, and we shared our goals out loud with each other. Writing them down was a strong action, but speaking them out loud was even stronger. We asked questions to each other about our whys and hows for these goals. We praised each other for the time we took to write out those goals and to dream big, and for starting to make real plans to reach them. I know both of us left that meeting feeling empowered. Yes, we were encouraged by each other, but we felt empowered by our own actions to start bettering our lives. We were taking control, and that felt good.

After that, my process involved opening the notebook every night before bed and rereading every goal, every reason, and every way I planned to reach those goals. Every night, even if it was just a quick scan over the pages. It's amazing how easily my brain would forget how important something was to me, and that daily reminder helped me think about what I was going to do the next day to focus on my goals and be better tomorrow. Adding whys and hows to the pages every so often was amazing for keeping me focused on my goals. I know now that if I can't remind myself why I am doing something, then I just won't do it. Since starting that notebook, keeping track of my goals, and revisiting them often, my life has completely changed. Feeling in control and taking charge of my life has reduced my stress and added an incredible amount of joy, including finding joy in teaching again. I have simplified and organized my life and worked hard to maintain that order, and it has resulted in an all-around better life. I feel better about myself, and I know that I alone have control over my life. If I want something to be different, I can and will make it different. I stopped being a victim of my circumstances and fought for what I wanted because I knew that if I stayed focused and took one day, one step, one moment at a time, it would all work out.

When you hit rock bottom, the only way to go is up. It's hard because it may be easier to stay in that place. Getting up and out of burnout and out of that feeling of "stuckness" takes time, effort, and planning. But the results are worth the hard work. *You* are worth the work it takes to become a happier, healthier, more fulfilled human being.

HACK 8

N: NEVER SETTLE FOR A BURNED-OUT CAREER AND LIFE
PREPARE FOR HARDSHIP BY KEEPING YOUR GOALS AND ACTION STEPS IN MIND

The future belongs to those who prepare for it today.
— MALCOLM X, MINISTER AND ACTIVIST

THE PROBLEM: YOU'RE NOT MENTALLY PREPARED FOR CRISIS OR HARDSHIP

DO YOU WEAR a seatbelt?

Do you participate in fire/safety drills at school?

Do you have a savings account?

Do you have toilet paper stored in your house?

Hopefully, your answer to these questions is, "Of course I do!" If not, then you have yet to realize that it's not a question of *if* there will be a hardship, it's a question of when. I don't need to remind you, as educators, of the challenges you've faced in the past and warn you of the hardships to come in your future.

Being prepared for the not-so-great things that may come your way might seem a little doomsday; however, you must prepare to be part of the future, and this includes taking a proactive stance against whatever life may throw your way.

Preparing for hardship will help you:

- Eliminate overwhelm

- Create clarity when life gets a little foggy

- Stay focused during good times and bad

- Support your established priorities

- Initiate lasting change to reach your goals

> ONCE YOU MOVE THROUGH EACH STAGE AND OUT OF BURNOUT, YOU'LL KNOW HOW TO START THIS PROCESS OVER AGAIN WHENEVER YOU FACE LARGE OR SMALL CHALLENGES. YOU NOW KNOW HOW TO AVOID SETTLING.

Do those sound familiar? They should, because we've been discussing the need for elimination, creation, help, support, and encouragement throughout this book.

When you're deep in burnout, you don't see the point in setting goals. As you've moved through these Hacks, you now have all the tools you need to define, reflect, and act on your teacher burnout. If you don't have goals, if you aren't pushing yourself, and if you aren't taking daily action (even if they are small actions), then you are settling and are not preparing for a lifestyle of empowerment, joy, and balance for what matters most to you. You need goals and action to avoid settling back into the trenches that led you to the burned-out stage in the first place.

Someone may have told you to be content and grateful for what you have and accept things the way they are. However, you may later be told not to settle (hence the title of this Hack). But there's a huge difference between contentment, acceptance, and settling. If you're not prepared for hardship, you're virtually guaranteed to settle for a life where, when crisis and hardship happen, you become a victim of your lack of preparation.

Avoid settling and setting yourself up for failure. Instead, plan to get yourself out of burnout and do what it takes to make that happen.

THE HACK: NEVER SETTLE FOR A BURNED-OUT CAREER AND LIFE

Now you know more about how to handle any crisis or hardship that comes your way. You know what it means if (or, likely, when) you find yourself on the edge or stuck deep in burnout again.

Settling versus radical acceptance versus contentment

Contentment means to feel satisfied and pleased. This is what we're all striving for, right? Don't we all have the right to life, liberty, and the pursuit of happiness? In essence, that's the real goal of beating burnout: being content in the life that you're living.

Remember when we talked about radical acceptance? It's about accepting certain experiences happening around you, such as how a child is being raised or the way a principal is running a school— even though they're not doing it the way you see as acceptable or even right. Radical acceptance also applies to the policies that schools and teachers must follow, and we may not have control over those policies. If you choose not to make it your mission in life to change these policies, or to run a school, or to advocate for children as your career, you simply have to accept those things the way they are and focus on your profession, your core values, and your people.

Brooke Castillo, a life coach, says settling includes activities such as continuing to do what we know isn't in our best interest, without doing any evaluation or thought work; willingly staying in a negative emotion or consciously giving up; or shortchanging ourselves by not moving away from what feels bad. For instance, staying at a school or district that you know isn't right for you because you're scared of what it would mean to try something new or go to a different school—even if you know it would mean being more valued—is settling.

The good news is, if you refuse to settle, you'll arm yourself with the eight steps to go from isolated to empowered. By following the process, you can overcome any challenge. Once you move through each stage and out of burnout, you'll know how to start this process over again whenever you face large or small challenges, and, of course, burnout. You now have a cyclical system for solving your burnout or any struggles you face in or out of education. You now know how to avoid settling.

WHAT **YOU** CAN DO TOMORROW

- **Show grace.** You're working in a building full of people who rely on you from the top and the bottom. You aren't pushing buttons on a machine every day. You're dealing with people, and people bring a lot of baggage, personalities, bias, and expectations. Everyone is fighting a battle, and we don't know the reasons people (children or adults) do what they do. When you're in a position where it's easy to get angry and say hurtful things, choose grace instead.

- **Choose kindness.** Hardships may show up in the form of outbursts against us, well-intentioned but not well-planned initiatives, and even intentional mean comments or acts. When you have a choice between being right and being kind, choose to be kind.

- **Know the difference between self-care and self-indulgence.** Self-care is not selfish. Self-care is taking care of your needs like getting enough sleep, staying hydrated, going to the doctor when necessary, eating when you're hungry, using the bathroom when you need to, exercising, staying connected to people you love, and keeping yourself clean and healthy, overall.

  Self-care is also the hard stuff like difficult conversations, saying no, or advocating for yourself and others.

  Self-indulgences are fun and rewarding, and we need to include them in our lives occasionally for optimal well-being. These include getting a massage, getting your nails done, buying a splurge item, or enjoying private you-time once a week (such as a bubble bath and a glass of wine, or an evening in the man-cave while watching a favorite show). You know, the activities that many people photograph and post on social media, making it look like these splurges represent their daily lives. But we know how to filter through the filtered photos, don't we?

It's valuable to know the difference between self-care and self-indulgence; to avoid settling into burnout again, we must know how to take care of ourselves first. Practicing self-care takes work, vision, planning, daily discipline, and intention.

A BLUEPRINT FOR FULL IMPLEMENTATION

STEP 1: Begin where you are.

You're already further along in your journey than you were before you started, so as you reflect, you won't have to travel back as far as you did the first time. You also know how to assess what type of burnout you are experiencing and what stage you're in, and you have specific action steps that you can take to tackle your challenges.

STEP 2: Understand your teacher brand.

At this point, I encourage you to work on a teacher brand you can be proud of, and as you grow and continue to gain clarity around your core values, people, and goals, you may need to adjust your brand. And that's okay. You know what steps to take to evaluate and improve your brand.

STEP 3: Reflect on your challenges.

You now have the ability to:

- Assess what's challenging you.
- Decide whether you can control it or not.
- If you can control it, take action and face it.

STEP 4: Nurture your strengths and habits.

You know your greatest strengths that you carry with you every day. What are they? Write them, read them, and say them out loud. Are you using them? Is it time for a change? Are you letting habits that keep you at your best fall to the wayside?

STEP 5: Extend your reach and possibilities.

If you have gone back to mindless movie binging or having the same old conversations that aren't stimulating your brain or challenging your thinking, maybe it's time to turn off Netflix and turn on a podcast. Or perhaps it's time to plug into a professional learning network. The point is, push yourself to keep growing.

STEP 6: Determine your long-term goals.

If you have lost sight of what you want, revisit the goals you listed in Hack 6 and center yourself again. Show yourself grace and move forward. Always move forward.

STEP 7: Initiate lasting change.

How long has it been since you documented your Word of the Year, goals, and action steps? Did you go too hard and get road rash? Remember, taking time to rest is a good thing. You can't be going,

going, going all the time. Be diligent about balancing productivity with personal growth and joy to sustain your positive changes.

STEP 8: Never settle for burnout again.

Of course, never settle for living an unfulfilled, overwhelmed, anxious, or frustrated life. You only get one life, so why not fill it with joy, laughter, action, and growth? Work takes work, and life takes living. Never settle for a life that you're just "surviving" your way through. Thrive.

OVERCOMING PUSHBACK

I don't love teaching anymore. This book's goal isn't to make you "love teaching" again or make you feel like you have to stay where you are in your career and life, unless that's what you want. The process I've laid out for you is to help you along your path of self-awareness and self-discovery. Of course, we don't want teachers interacting with kids when those teachers hate the profession or the content they're presenting. We need educators who like what they do most days and project their love of learning and growth onto their students. If you don't love teaching, then it's up to you to determine what you want to do. It's okay to acknowledge that you're ready to grow into another role, in or out of the classroom.

I realize that my reason for burnout has a lot to do with my personal life. What do I do? It is virtually impossible for a human being to build a strong wall between work and home life. Of course, at times, you have to focus on one over the other. Even wonderful life situations, like a new marriage or a new baby, can cause stress and challenges in your work life. Likewise, taking on a new role at a new district may also cause challenges in your personal life.

Suppose you've gone through the steps in this book, only

to realize that your personal life is full of consistent challenges and causing you so much stress, anxiety, and frustration that it's ruining what used to be a happy, fulfilling career. In that case, I encourage you to make sure that your personal life matches up with your core values, mission statement, strengths, habits, and goals. If not, then just like in any career, you can choose to take or not take steps to make your life happier and more fulfilling.

You're 100 percent responsible for your life. So begin where you are, and focus on your personal life first if that's what you need to do. I guarantee this process will help you there too.

THE HACK IN ACTION
By Janelle O. and Angela R., classroom teachers

Time. Time was a constant issue. Not enough time to plan, grade, collaborate, or respond to email at school. We spent too much time at school after contractual time to work. Even that was not enough time! So we robbed time at home to complete those tasks. We spent time after dinner, before bed, and even on the weekends to do what we could not do during school hours. We had to answer emails from administrators, colleagues, students, and parents as soon as possible to make sure the people sending them knew the answers or had the information they needed to continue with their tasks. We felt constant pressure to get everything done so that others remained happy. This situation came at a huge price: family time and personal care. We constantly felt guilty that we didn't spend enough meaningful time during the school year with the very people who should get the bulk of our attention: our families.

This scenario is the cost of being a teacher, right? But the guilt and stress that came from a constant need for more time led us down a short path to burnout.

It became apparent that we had a serious need to evaluate how to set goals and prioritize work. This reflection led to an understanding that we needed to change our mindsets. To a certain degree, we are in control of our time, and we need to take back that control.

We realized that nobody was telling us we had to be available by email twenty-four hours a day, seven days a week. We had put that on ourselves. So we set aside time during the school day to devote to reading and responding to email. We allowed ourselves to redefine "urgent" and recognize that responding within twenty-four hours to non-urgent emails was realistic. We set boundaries for when to stop checking email, even turning off school email notifications on our cell phones and hiding the email app in a folder.

To better organize our time during the school day, we implemented dump pages to write down every needed task. This process allowed us to prioritize tasks and time allotment to get things done and helped to reduce the bad habit of jumping from one task to another during prep, which meant finishing nothing. We also discovered that we could do quick tasks (organizing papers and assessing small assignments) while students worked independently or during small group work time. We enjoyed the amazing feeling that came with crossing items off of the never-ending to-do list.

Because of staying organized at school, we felt less of a demand to work at home in the evenings or on the weekends. Did it eliminate it? Not completely. However, much of the stress and over-working eased once we started these habits.

During this time of virtual teaching, it is easy to misstep and fall back into previous habits, because we are not in a school building and classroom. At home, we have families and different priorities and obligations.

So what to do? Go back to the basics.

Make lists. Make a separate list for home and school. Prioritize. Think ahead to the next week and place items on next week's lists (especially tasks that can wait). Feel the reward of crossing off items from the list.

Set a hard stop time. The work will be there the next day. No email or ungraded paper or planning needs to rob you of your afternoon and evening—especially since that is your family and self-time.

Prioritize your personal well-being and family time. We are individuals and spouses and parents—first. Stress and change are a part of life: they're unavoidable. But never settle. Knowing how to handle those events with purposeful actions and responses will ease the fear and doubt that creep in, and it will put you back on track to a more fulfilled life.

Changing your story of what it means to be a good teacher takes time and practice. When you prioritize your well-being and goals above believing and doing what you were doing before, you can consistently grow your mindset to make your vision come into focus. You can let yourself see things for what they are: complicated. Never settle for the belief that good teachers always work. You can choose to believe that good teachers say no and set boundaries. And of course, good teachers accept that challenges will always be there, but continue to focus on solutions that are within their control.

CONCLUSION
YOU ARE CAPABLE AND WORTHY OF GETTING OUT OF BURNOUT

THE FIRST STEP to any change is believing you are capable and worthy of it. Your belief in yourself, your values, and your purpose will carry you through multitudes of future challenges and crises that are sure to come your way both in your personal and professional lives.

You may not have chosen to teach with "that teacher" or have "that student" in your class. You didn't choose to have your disability that makes it even harder to teach today's kids. You also didn't choose the policies that keep education in a constant state of push and pull.

You can choose to take control of the one thing that only changes when you decide to change it: your beliefs about your capability and worthiness to live a life that brings you happiness and joy—no matter what. Making this choice doesn't mean you slap on a smile when you're hurting. It doesn't mean that you ignore your suffering. It means you are vulnerable and brave enough to acknowledge your hurt and suffering and move through these steps again.

Use these eight steps repeatedly. Go through them again and again, whenever you need to center yourself and focus on dealing with any challenge or crisis. Whether someone intentionally hurts you or you find yourself in a situation where you can't feel or do your best, come back to these steps and begin where you are. Think about how long this challenge has been triggering feelings of frustration or anxiety. Then remember your core values and who your people are. Centering yourself and coming back there first and foremost will allow you to focus on your next, best, imperfect step.

BEING A BURNED-IN TEACHER IS ALL ABOUT MOVING FORWARD, FOCUSING ON SOLUTIONS, AND BELIEVING YOU ARE CAPABLE AND WORTHY OF A LIFE WHERE YOU FEEL POWERFUL AND IN CONTROL OF THE ONE THING THAT CAN CHANGE YOUR REALITY DURING ANY CHALLENGE: YOU.

And that's what being a BURNED-IN teacher is all about: moving forward, focusing on solutions, and believing you are capable and worthy of a life where you feel powerful and in control of the one thing that can change your reality during any challenge: you.

As you continually move through this process each time you feel challenged, you will watch others struggle in isolation—just like you did. You will see teachers fighting the same battles and beliefs that you once did. Now you can become an advocate for them and share your story of transformation. They may choose to listen and ask questions, or they may choose not to. Their journey is theirs, and yours is yours. But continue to show up, check in, and offer support.

When you choose to show up with a plan of action for yourself and others when life gets hard, you are on fire for teaching and for life. You've empowered yourself with the tools to believe you are capable and worthy of solutions within your control and to empower others to believe the same. That's how the process continues from isolation to empowerment, and the fire grows for a happy and fulfilling career and life.

Burn on.

EPILOGUE

*T*HIS EPILOGUE OFFERS *a closing bookend to the Pro-logue. It completes Val's story and shares how this book relates to these times.*

Val was ready to throw in the teaching towel, but she decided to Hack Teacher Burnout during the Coronavirus pandemic and then see how she felt.

School was out for the summer, and Val didn't know what the next school year would hold, but she did know one thing: life had to change, and she began with herself. She followed the eight steps of the BURNED-IN Teacher process.

She decided that her core values were *family* and *acceptance*. Her people for the summer were her children and husband, and she started to create boundaries to protect her time with them.

She set aside times in her day to interact with friends, extended family, and colleagues via phone, social media, or Zoom. She left her phone plugged-in in her bedroom for most of the day while she played with the kids or worked on projects that she and Jeff decided to complete to help their home be more organized and comfortable for their family. No more piling papers on the kitchen table for Jeff. No more leaving dirty dishes in the sink. And the "catch-all" room with toys and outgrown clothes turned into a home office as a quieter place for Jeff or Val to use for work.

Val sent out an email to her principal and her closest colleagues, asking them what words they would use to describe her, and most of them replied with kind and patient—which made her feel amazing. However, the words stressed and tired showed up, too, which only validated what she already felt. So, she worked on ways to adjust her daily schedule to get more rest and to eliminate activities she used to do because she told herself that "good moms and good teachers do these things." She started checking email twice a day instead of all day—twenty minutes in the morning and twenty minutes in the evening. She also turned off all notifications on her phone and removed email from her phone entirely.

She resigned from three of the five committees and clubs that she was a part of and created space in her calendar and head to focus on her values. And speaking of her calendar, she started sticking to it religiously: no more being surprised by unscheduled events or requests, except occasional emergencies, of course.

She and Jeff set aside time each week to talk about what caused stress between them. She also talked with the kids about helping around the house, especially on weekends, to prepare for the week ahead—yes, even during the summer. They had family conversations about routines and new habits.

Lastly, she accepted that she was one person and could only hold some of the weight of her students' success on her shoulders.

She would continue to be kind and patient, but no longer bear the burden of what she could not change. At the end of last school year, she connected with twenty out of twenty-eight of her students, and while she wished she had reached them all, she understood that she tried, and that had to be enough.

She also accepted that the next school year would be more challenging, with processes she may not like, agree with, or want to do. However, because she worked through the eight steps with smaller challenges that arose in the summer, she built habits to help her better handle the hardships that will inevitably come her way. That's life. But she felt empowered with the belief that she is in control of herself. And she had the goals and the drive to help her reach them.

She decided not to settle for anything less than choosing happiness in this one life she has and is so grateful to live. For the first time, she felt grounded in her beliefs about her worthiness and capability to grow and change.

ABOUT THE AUTHOR

Amber Harper taught for twelve years in the elementary school classroom and now works as a Teacher Burnout Coach and Google Trainer in Northeast Indiana. While teaching full time, she created BURNED-IN Teacher, a website and community dedicated to helping teachers. She began leading Google Training Workshops for her local and state Education Service Centers and schools in 2016. Amber hosts a weekly podcast called The Burned-In Teacher Podcast, which is one-part burnout and all other parts action, inspiration, and support for teachers. She is part of the Education Podcast Network, where she serves educators through professional and personal development.

Amber is passionate about helping teachers stop the isolation and shame associated with burnout. Her mission is to activate teacher self-empowerment by teaching and coaching through her eight-step process. She's taking what she learned through her experiences as a classroom teacher, her research, and her work with hundreds of burned-out teachers to create a movement of empowered educators. Amber empowers them with the strategies, mental strength, and renewed passion for taking their next best steps to become BURNED-IN educators.

She leads in-person workshops and shares keynote speeches, sharing her proven process to help teachers beat burnout and live a happier, more fulfilled life.

Connect with Amber:

support@burnedinteacher.com

burnedinteacher.com

community.burnedinteacher.com

Twitter, Instagram, and LinkedIn: @burnedinteacher

Facebook: facebook.com/burnedinteacher

ACKNOWLEDGMENTS

If you want to go fast, go alone. If you
want to go far, go together.

— AFRICAN PROVERB

To EVERYONE WHO has listened to my dream and supported this journey, thank you.

To my family:

Jeff, Hannah, and Avery—you have been so patient and willing to offer me the time and space it takes to build something from the ground up to help thousands of people who we don't know, but know need help. You've even been more patient with me as I've put everything into writing for *Hacking Teacher Burnout*. Thank you for encouraging me to dream and fail and keep trying anyway.

To all teachers and administrators I've ever worked with:

This book is because of and for you. I remember so many of our interactions, and I don't take them for granted. The lessons I've learned from you are priceless, and not a day goes by that I don't use something I've learned from one of you to remind myself or others that "people will forget what you said and what you did, but people will never forget how you made them feel" (Maya Angelou).

To my Top Five Influencers:

You know who you are, because I often remind you how grateful

I am for your support, feedback, and continued encouragement. You inspire me to be a better version of myself with each of your responses to my texts, DMs, emails, Voxes, or Marco Polos. I can't imagine my vision coming to be and impacting so many lives without your influence. Thank you for encouraging me to use my own strategies when I slip into a fixed and scarcity mindset, and reminding me that this work is for all of us when we feel isolated and need someone in our corner to help us feel empowered.

To the Times 10 Publications team:

As daunting and scary as it was to dedicate myself and my time to this incredible challenge, I can't imagine that it could have been easier than you all have made it. Mark and Jennifer, working with you was a dream, and I'm so grateful that I have had the opportunity to work with you and the rest of the Times 10 team to bring this book to the teachers who need it most.

BURNED-IN TEACHER RESOURCES

To learn more about your burnout type and stage, take the Teacher Burnout Quiz at burnedinteacher.com/burnoutquiz.

Download and print out the Agents of Change posters at burnedinteacher.com/agentsofchange, and refer to them anytime you need to take control of your self-talk and work toward more productive and positive ways to talk to yourself.

Choose one of the following online personality tests to learn more about yourself:

- 16personalities.com/free-personality-test

- truity.com/test/enneagram-personality-test

- gallup.com/cliftonstrengths/en/ (purchase the book, which contains a code to take the test)

MORE FROM TIMES 10

Browse our library at 10Publications.com

Browse our library at 10Publications.com

Browse our library at 10Publications.com

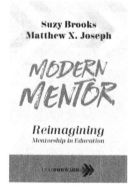

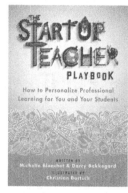

Browse our library at 10Publications.com

Browse our library at 10Publications.com

RESOURCES FROM TIMES 10

10Publications.com

Join the Times 10 Ambassadors and help us revolutionize education:

10Publications.com/ambassador

Podcasts:

hacklearningpodcast.com

jamesalansturtevant.com/podcast

On Twitter:

@10Publications

@HackMyLearning

#Times10News

@LeadForward2

#LeadForward

#HackLearning

#HackingLeadership

#MakeWriting

#HackingQs

#HackingSchoolDiscipline

#LeadWithGrace

#QuietKidsCount

#ModernMentor

#AnxiousBook

All things Times 10:

10Publications.com

Vision, Experience, Action
10PUBLICATIONS.COM

TIMES 10 is helping all education stakeholders improve every aspect of teaching and learning. We are committed to solving big problems with simple ideas. We bring you content from experts, shared through books, podcasts, and an array of social networks. Our books bring Vision, Experience, and Action to educators around the world. Stay in touch with us at 10Publications.com and follow our updates on Twitter @10Publications and #Times10News.

Made in the USA
Monee, IL
10 June 2022

97827945R00115